Successful Moms
OF THE BIBLE

Katara Washington Patton

New York Boston Nashville

FaithWords
Hachette Book Group
1290 Avenue of the Americas
New York, NY 10104
faithwords.com
twitter.com/faithwords

First Edition: April 2016

FaithWords is a division of Hachette Book Group, Inc.
The FaithWords name and logo are trademarks of Hachette Book Group, Inc.

The publisher is not responsible for websites (or their content) that are not owned by the publisher.

The Hachette Speakers Bureau provides a wide range of authors for speaking events. To find out more, go to www.hachettespeakersbureau.com or call (866) 376-6591.

Scripture quotations labeled NIV are from the Holy Bible, New International Version®. NIV®. Copyright © 1973, 1978, 1984, 2011 by Biblica, Inc.™ Used by permission of Zondervan. All rights reserved worldwide. www.zondervan.com

Scripture quotations labeled NLT are from the Holy Bible, New Living Translation, copyright © 1996, 2004, 2007 by Tyndale House Foundation. Used by permission of Tyndale House Publishers, Inc., Carol Stream, Illinois 60188. All rights reserved.

Scripture quotations labeled MSG are from *The Message* by Eugene H. Peterson, copyright © 1993, 1994, 1995, 2000, 2001, 2002. Used by permission of NavPress Publishing Group. All rights reserved.

Scriptures noted KJV are taken from the King James Version of the Bible.

Library of Congress Control Number: 2015960360

ISBNs: 978-1-4555-3884-3 (trade pbk.), 978-1-4555-3883-6 (ebook)

Printed in the United States of America

RRD-C

10 9 8 7 6 5 4 3 2 1

This book is dedicated to the absolute best mom a girl could have—Ernestine C. Washington (1942–2006). Mom, you may not be here with me physically, but everything I do, say, think, write as a woman of faith and as a mother has been influenced by your amazing example. I'm forever grateful for the mom you were to me, Kenneth, and Kim. You and Daddy gave us your all. Thank you.

Contents

Introduction   1

Mary   5
    Successful moms pray and hold on to God's
    promises so they can serve, nurture, and
    develop their children.

Jochebed   23
    Successful moms protect their kids—at all costs.

Hannah   37
    Successful moms always pray for their kids—
    from conception through adulthood.

Abigail   51
    Successful moms are wise examples to their
    children.

Sarah   63
    Successful moms balance faith in God
    and action.

Elizabeth   75
   Successful moms believe the impossible—
   no matter how long it takes.

Rebekah   89
   Successful moms know their own issues—
   and don't let them become their kids' issues.

Leah   103
   Successful moms don't use their kids as pawns
   in their love life.

Ruth   117
   Successful moms utilize their village to raise
   their children.

Proverbs 31 Woman   131
   Putting it all together—a collage of successful
   moms.

Acknowledgments   147

Successful Moms
OF THE BIBLE

Introduction

When I was growing up, my mom often said everything I needed to know about life was in the Bible. She called the Bible a manual for living. Because I observed her faith and life up close and personal, I know she believed this statement and lived her life always looking for God's answer in the Bible. But when I grew up, got married, and had a child of my own, one of the first things I heard was that kids didn't come with a handbook. While there was plenty of information on pregnancy, what to expect at each stage of child development, and a boatload of books on raising kids, there was still a sense of adventure and fear of the unknown among my mommy friends. We gathered together often to talk about the latest developments and wondered what to do next—often googling a phrase just to see what would come up (after all, that was how I had handled every symptom I had had during pregnancy).

Then I got to thinking: what if the Bible has the answers? I took my mom's advice and opened up the pages of the Bible in search of answers on being a successful mom, teaching my child about life, handling bullies, balancing this mommyhood thing, and so much more. I reread some of the stories of moms of the Bible—and I'm happy to report that my mom was absolutely right. We have lots to learn from the pages of scriptures and what they say about moms of the Bible.

If we open our eyes and hearts, we can hear the moms of the Bible teaching us invaluable lessons about raising our kids. Some things have changed—thank God—but for the most part, we—just like the women of antiquity in the Bible—all want the best for our children and take this special task of mommyhood seriously.

I hope you will journey with me as I retell the stories of some of my favorite—and successful—moms of the Bible and gather real, motherly advice on raising children. Whether you are expecting or nursing a baby or caring for a toddler, tween, or teenager, these women have something to share to encourage you on this journey. Or perhaps you've successfully raised or mentored children who are now adults; I bet you can still relate to these women and the challenges they faced and overcame.

Motherhood is not for the weak. It takes guts to raise children well and still keep ourselves intact. We need more than a firm hand and a special, authoritative look; we need wisdom and help. God has placed all we need inside of our manual—the Bible—and as we unpack the messages shared from the moms in the Bible, we will garner the support we need. Take a seat and soak in the stories of our foremothers so you can gain new strength for the motherhood journey.

God has called us to this special task—and has left us with special help and messages. Let's acquire some motherly wisdom.

Mary

Successful moms pray and hold on
to God's promises so they can serve,
nurture, and develop their children.

Motherhood changes you, there is no doubt about it.
From the first moment you suspect you might be carrying
a child, to the moment you see the ultrasound picture that
resembles a strange, alien-looking being, to the moment
of the birth, and for every single moment thereafter,
a woman's life is changed when she becomes a mother.
And even when a woman becomes a mom through adoption or via the village concept, she too is forever changed.
Motherhood, somehow, opens your heart in a way I can't
explain. It's as if caring for another expands your capacity
for love and somehow makes you caretaker of all, if only
in your soul. And this larger, more open heart exposes you
to all sorts of concerns, worry, and scenarios you never

would have thought of in a million years. Yes, motherhood changes you.

Somehow, within an instant, we go from frolicking carefree through life to worrying about everything. *Did I buckle the seat belt? Is the car seat even installed correctly?* "Is she still breathing?" you ask as you tiptoe into the room. You know the silent monitor is probably working—but you really need to see your child's stomach rise up and down to confirm that your precious one is still alive. You don't want to wake him up—no mom ever wants to wake a sleeping child. (After all, naps have got to be special gifts from God, a little message reminding us that our Lord is indeed merciful!) As the precious child grows to a not-so-precious teen, you still worry—perhaps even more. Is she texting while driving—or tuning the radio or talking to her friends— instead of watching the road? What if his friends offer him drugs? Or what if the bully...? Moms worry!

Motherhood Changes Us

Motherhood changes us! A friend once told me she had prayed all her life, but during the first year of her marriage, she had prayed more than she had prayed in all her previous years combined. I laughed. But then, I got married and I prayed. And when I had our first child, my prayer life expanded even more. From the beginning, I prayed for God to cover our child and protect our child and for our child to grow healthily, know God's love, make lifelong friends, and love school and her teachers and…

Motherhood calls you to pray more and pray often. We can finally get 1 Thessalonians 5:17 down. "Pray without ceasing" (KJV) or, as the New Living Translation says: "Never stop praying"! The writer of Thessalonians must have been close to some moms when he wrote that verse, because motherhood makes you pray—all the time. It's really the only way we juggle the overwhelming task of mommyhood with the crazy mission called life!

But there's a mother in the Bible who doesn't look as frazzled as my mom friends and I do discussing the latest issues while keeping one eye on our children during their playdate. (Aren't playdates another blessing?!) There's someone who was called to raise a king, the Savior, our Lord, and she looks pretty calm every time I see her in the Bible. You know her as Mary, mother of Jesus. I see her as a model of peace and tranquility in the midst of craziness— and I mean real craziness. Oh, Mary? Please tell us how you did that. Your life was interrupted and changed forever when the angel Gabriel appeared and made that announcement, but still you took it all in stride (Luke 1:26–28).

Mary, a Beacon of Wisdom

I don't see Mary fighting to get Jesus into the best day care program because that will lead to selective enrollment in the top kindergarten, which leads to the best college! (Huh?! Really, the method you use to teach our children their colors determines their future college admissions? And the price tag for those early-childhood programs could very well pay for an Ivy League college education!) I don't see Mary stressing over how many kids to invite to her son's birthday party—or even the venue—and scheduling it four months in advance and preparing just the right take-home goodie bags. (What happened to parties where cake and ice cream were enough and playing pin the tail on the donkey was a really big deal?!) I don't see Mary working late at night to create yet another class project or filling out college applications for her children because she's afraid they won't make the deadline and they'll never get into any other school and then their lives will spiral downward and...No, when I look at scripture, I see a totally different picture of motherhood in Mary. She doesn't seem fazed by the clarion call of mommyhood. She isn't cloaked in worry—the by-product of attempting to maintain control over every iota of her children's lives—like most moms I know. What I see when I see Mary is calmness and peace, a demeanor that eludes today's soccer moms.

Studying Mother Mary teaches us how to raise children in a crazy and cruel world. She is a beacon of wisdom and demonstrates the attitude moms need in order to navigate through the overwhelmingness of mommyhood while crazily trying to do life at the same time.

How do you do it, Mary? How can you be so calm while raising kids—while raising Jesus? Please share.

Piecing together Mary's story throughout scripture may give us moms some clues.

Like us, Mary's life changed immediately once she heard those words: "Congratulations, you're pregnant!" The *Message* translation actually says it more accurately. It records that the angel Gabriel showed up, greeted Mary, and said, "God has a surprise for you" (Luke 1:29–33). Now, that's a line for every mom to remember: God has a surprise for you! And yeah, while Mary's surprise was a little more surprising than any mother's I know—that producing-a-child-*before*-having-sex part— I believe that line is still true for every woman whose life is changed by nurturing and caring for a child: *God has a surprise for you!* Now Mary did have a few questions for Gabriel when he thrust that news upon her—and who could blame the woman?! I can hear her asking, *How is this so? I've never been with a man. Oh my, what will Joseph say?*

Whether God has chosen you to be the mother of the Savior or of a president, a teacher, or the next person who will grow up and show love and care to another (you know your child has all of that potential bottled up inside her little body or teenaged heart), apparently learning that you've been called to the sacred task of motherhood puts you in a new mode. You are forever changed. You know you are called to serve and nurture and care for someone precious, even more precious than yourself.

What a daunting task. What a surprise God has for you!

Mothers Are True Servants

Mary shows us how to handle this amazingly awesome task. It's almost as if she took in every word dear Gabriel had to say, processed them rather quickly, and came up with her wise conclusion. Mary hears the angel Gabriel, in all his lofty language. She hears his words and knows he means more. I can hear her wondering, *So, yeah, Gabriel, you say I'm going to have a child—even though I haven't been with a man yet? This must be some child, some miracle. And what if, just what if, I were to believe you and think I would produce the Savior of the world this way... may I ask, why me? I'm not noble, I'm not the prettiest. I haven't even been the best. I'm just a little country girl trying to get through this life. I have someone who wants to marry me and I think we can settle down and have a good life. But, you say, it's going to be a lot different than we've dreamed, huh?*

Within just a few moments, Mary continues to take in this life-changing news: *I know Joseph's a good man, but come on... you think he's going to believe I got pregnant miraculously? Yes, you say. Well, let me tell you one thing—*

I'm going to have to let you and the good Lord handle that one. If you say Joseph will go for it, great, but you're going to have to make that one work out on your own. I already know there are some things in this life I just can't deal with—so that one is on you and God, Angel Gabe.

Gabriel returns with: *Don't worry, Mary. This is just the beginning. Your motherhood journey is going to be one for the books. The Almighty God knows motherhood is no easy road, but God is going to surprise you, my dear. You are going to be amazed by the child God gives you. You're going to be filled with wonder at everything he does—and blessed by what he ultimately does for the entire world. And, just for the record, I like your attitude. Remember to let God handle that really tough and perplexing stuff—you don't need to understand everything if you're willing to trust God.*

And almost instantly after she gets out those questions Mary accepts the news of her pending parenthood and says, *Okay, I'm up for this. I'm God's servant. How do I get started?*

Mary was a wise chick. Clearly, she understood—more than many of us—that one big part of motherhood is service. From changing diapers, to wiping off spit-up and washing and washing and washing clothes, to carpooling and shuffling around town to baseball and tennis and swimming and ballet and piano and birthday parties (oh, the birthday parties), to cooking vegetables and cutting them in cute shapes in hopes that someone, anyone, will eat them and grow up to have strong bones and healthy teeth...yes, healthy, nonexpensive teeth! Mary accepted that mommyhood meant taking a backseat in your own home, going without so your children can have. Staying up late and rising early—all in the name of the children. She understood that servanthood was a huge part of this mommy thing. And she openly and gladly accepted it.

Whoa, mother of God! She should be considered a saint...no joking. Many moms, myself included, still struggle with the *servant* word. We love our kids, Lord knows we do, but do they have to need us all the time? Do you really need to call my name one more time? Can I just use the bathroom in peace or talk to my girl pal for fifteen uninterrupted minutes? (I really do miss talking to her—ever since she was blessed with her first child nearly fourteen years ago!) Just one moment is all we crave, just one—without the threat of returning to find paint on the walls and the one precious figurine from Aunt Claire broken! Can I get one moment, please? Um, no, you're a servant now! *God has a surprise for you.*

I think when we begin to see ourselves as Mary saw herself, as a servant of God, we can handle those duties with a little more grace and patience. We are in essence working for God, tending to the souls and care of the little ones and the older ones in our charge. This mommyhood thing is a sacred task, and we have been assigned to it. In all its glory and in all its messiness, we have been selected and chosen to be called mother.

• • •

Okay, I see myself as a servant now, a servant of God, called to nourish and guide and lead this one toward adulthood, independence, citizenship...Yes! Our task is no slight one; there is no greater calling. But how can I, like Mary, break out into the Magnificat (Mary's praise song in Luke 1:46–55) because of what God has done, because God has chosen me to serve these particular children?

Still Mary teaches. One of the first things she does— after she questions Gabriel and accepts life as a servant of God but even before she can sing her praise song—is to run to be in the company of another woman who is pregnant with possibility and whose prayer has been answered (Luke 1:39–40). Mary wants to rejoice with a woman who understands her condition.

Know Where You Can Find Support

When the young Mary first found out the news, she ran straight to her older cousin Elizabeth, who was also carrying a miracle baby. Scripture says Mary stayed three months in the company of this older cousin. Mary was hanging out with another promise-bearer; she was soaking up the awesomeness of God, bathing in the beauty of answered prayers and the sacred call to servanthood. She knew where to hang out; she didn't run through the streets sharing her good news with everyone—not just yet. She ran to the side of someone she knew would understand her and support her and rejoice with her (and this person wasn't her husband-to-be; sometimes our dear mates just don't understand the magnitude of motherhood!). Oh, the joy of having supportive sisters and aunts and moms who can rejoice with us even when life seems strange and daunting and overwhelming. Do you know whom you can call or text or visit when you need this type of care? Keep that woman on speed dial and use her number as often as possible! She can somehow remind you about the awesomeness of this task. Yes, even though you're buried in homework and tournament schedules, another mom— a sister in solidarity—can remind you of your ultimate task: to serve these kids. You can see the joy in her eyes— most days. You can be reminded of the calling because of the joy she has. You can see God's promise when you look at her. Keep her close. Keep her near. Hang on to her for dear life. No one knows what you're going through quite like another mommy.

Your Elizabeth could be the woman who knows you're overwhelmed by the look in your eyes. Even while you have a smile on your face, she can sense that you could use a break. She's the mom who drops by and says she'll sit with the kids while you go do anything else, even just sit in your car and catch your breath. Or she's the aunt who just happens to come by to take the kids out for pizza so you can catch a nap or clean or cook or do whatever.

Or that friend who sends the text at the right moment: "You're a great mom." Ah, yes, someone sees and knows. Thank God for sisters who understand. Thank God for women who journey with you. Keep them close.

I still remember the sweet words of a mother I sit near in church most Sundays; she actually sits with her twenty-something-year-old grown daughters—a reminder to me that our kids actually do grow up! As I fretted over my nearly five-month-old precious child, this veteran mom reached over to hold her and whispered, "Sometimes you need a break too." Those little words made such a difference. She knew what I needed and she knew what I needed to hear. She went on to reminisce and educate me about how she had encouraged her husband to help more when her children were little and how she had laid out clothes for him to get the girls dressed in (already colored-coordinated, she explained with a smile). Had she looked into my home and observed my struggle? Moms just have a way of knowing. Keep your mommy support group close.

A Calm Mama

Another striking thing about Mary in scripture is her posture. If we had to put it in modern-day terms (or more like nineties terms), I'd call this mom cool, calm, and collected. She's not fretting or running around like a chicken with her head cut off. Mary, Mary doesn't seem contrary at all. Look at how she responds when Jesus goes missing (Luke 2:42–51)! She looks at him—after he's been missing for nearly three days—and asks him why he treated his dear parents in such a way. And when he answers, it seems as if she were saying, "Okay, let's carry on." Scripture says point-blank that she didn't really understand this man-child she was charged with raising. (Does anyone understand an adolescent boy or girl?!) But instead of throwing a temper tantrum at Jesus or making threats or reiterating all of the stress she's been under, Mary picks up and carries on. And that's not even the most admirable part of her story. Mary, our model of successful motherhood, stores what has happened in her heart. She holds the series of events "deep within herself," according to the *Message* translation.

Now, I'm thinking she didn't do what many of us would do—she didn't keep this incident in her heart and mind so she could bring it back up the next time a young Jesus did something stupid or displeasing to her. Mary, mother of God, stored this in her heart because she knew the incident, even with all the turmoil and confusion and anxiety it had caused, would point to his destiny. She knew somehow this behavior confirmed what she had been promised and told about her boy child way back when (Luke 2:17–18, 28–32, 38). Oh, to see the silly things they do, the hair-raising things these kids do, the OMG moments, as reminders of their destiny. To put things in their place and perspective even when emotions run amok is the mark of a wise, wise woman. Who has the grace and patience to sit by and really listen to why a child did something so crazy as getting lost in a crowd of people or running off to sit and listen at the temple? Mary, dear Mary, ponders what has happened. She sees the incident as yet another reminder of her amazing task—to nurture and raise Jesus. How can we see our children's inexcusable behavior or their back talk or fits as formation for their mission? How can we see God at work in every detail, every moment, every little annoying thing about our children? Oh, for the spirit of Mary.

Another review of scripture shows Mary pondering even more than talking. Mary ponders, rarely talks. She reflects and thinks about her sacred task often. She takes in everything. She hears it. She observes it. She sees it. Mary isn't missing a beat. She knows what is going on around her and her child. She hears the shepherds prophesying, speaking about what will become of this child. She witnesses Anna's and Simeon's proclamations (Luke 2:20–38)—strangers she encounters in the temple. Oh, she may not be shouting from the rooftops that she has the Savior, but she is well aware of what is happening...and she's storing the information in her heart. When Anna and Simeon proclaim greatness over the tiny tot presented in the temple, she soaks it in—not in a prideful, "look at how advanced my child is" way but in an "I've got to hang on to these words; these words will get me through" way.

How good are you at recalling the promises of God, Mommy? I know you had secret talks and conversations about motherhood, about your child, about the needs you faced. I know somehow God reassured you and told you things would be all right, but how often do you replay those sacred conversations and reminders? Do you ponder them when motherhood gets tough? When you've got to apply tough love? Do you remember the promises spoken over your child when he was just a tot? Or do you see only the wild teenager testing your patience today, breaking the rules and pushing her boundaries?

I want to be like Mary, always recalling the promises of God. I bet she even recalled that visit from Gabriel more than once. When an angel stops by to tell you God has a surprise for you, you don't easily forget that encounter! And I'm sure Mary was pondering the position God had put her in when Jesus was being talked about and set up for death (Mark 15:1–15). Mary needed to hang on to something. So she chose to hang on to the promise made to her early on. *You're going to have a surprise. You're going to raise the King of the kings, the Lord of lords. You, young lady, are going to be charged with nurturing someone great, someone who will make more than a difference in this world.*

Whew! What a task. How could she possibly do it without remembering all of God's promises and praying and reflecting and pondering?

Pondering and Praying

How can we do this motherhood thing without remembering our charge? It's a sacred task, never-ending and sometimes thankless, but still we have each been called to it. Whether it's raising a brood or one child or someone else's child, we have a sacred task to help raise the next generation. How can we do it without turning to God in prayer—constantly? How can we do it without renewing and remembering our charge, the surprise God had for us? Even if we tried and timed our little pregnancy to the *T*, it was still a surprise to see him form and develop and grow. Children are a miracle. The fact that we are called to tend to them is a miracle, a sweet surprise given to women by God.

I want to remember what the angel declared to Mary—and dare I say to every mom today: God has a surprise for you! It's not a trick; it's not even really a test—although we often think it is—it's a surprise, a joy, a good thing. It's a gift, a reminder that God has seen us and God has heard our prayers, spoken and unspoken. God has given us the desires of our hearts and we are entrusted to care for the souls of our kids. We are entrusted to raise them so they may live out their God-given mission. We are entrusted to guide them toward independence. What a gift. What a joy. Gosh, what a surprise.

We can be like Mary. We can be calm and sit and watch and listen as our kids grow and learn and bring forth the promises of God. When I put on my heart to ponder what God has told me about my child, I can push past the exhaustion and headaches and unending tasks and focus on nurturing and developing her—and enjoying her. When I remember that she is being groomed to be a leader, I can somehow weather her strong will a tad better. It might not make the smart mouth and sassy attitude go away, but I can be reminded that this child, this gift from God, was created for a special mission, and her mouth and attitude will be needed and used, I pray, for God's glory. Her strong opinions, while they need to be shaped and guided, will lead her toward success and help her stand up for herself at critical points in her life. I ponder like Mary that I've been given this gift of a child, and even when she is hurt by this world, both intentionally and unintentionally, I know God has plans to help her prosper and not to harm her (see Jeremiah 29:11). So, while it hurts to sit back and watch her get hurt, I can be like Mary and trust in God, trust in God's plan. After all, I'm a mom—a servant of God. I've been handpicked to guide this child at such a time as this. What a surprise God has for me.

I embrace motherhood each and every day, remembering and recalling God's promise made to me in the wee hours long ago when she was born and I was wondering how I would care for someone who wasn't even ten pounds. I recall the prayers sent up before she was conceived. I recall the people around my husband and me who surrounded us with blessings and gifts and showered us with prayers. I know those prayers were heard. I know God has plans for us. I recall scripture I've heard and read and I pray for the faith to transform mere words into real belief. And when I do, I can sit like Mary and smile and be thankful that God has looked upon me with favor and blessed me with this amazing surprise of a child.

I can get up early and go to bed late, check homework, shuttle to dance and piano lessons and to birthday parties, read one more book, and try very hard to wait patiently for my child to read the words I know she knows. And I can recall, I'm a mom—a servant of God. I may feel weary and tired and unappreciated sometimes, but still I'm a mom—a servant of God. I can do this.

I can be a Mary and ponder and observe—and you can too. Be slow to speak and even slower to react (see James 1:19). Give yourself a time-out to recall and remember and ponder. God has a surprise just for you, Mama!

—

My God and my Lord: Thank you for choosing me to be your servant, to nurture and raise the children you've given me. Give me a servant's heart, reminding me that I am serving you as I serve my family. I know you have a surprise for me every day. Help me to grab hold of all the wonderfulness of this task each step of the way. In your strength, I know I can do all you've called me to do. Amen.

Jochebed

*Successful moms protect their kids—
at all costs.*

Sometimes it takes a whole lot of guts—and confidence and courage and, dare I say, audacity—to be a mom. Given the right (or wrong) situation, we may have to put away our etiquette books and good-girl upbringing and do something radical, all in the name of saving our kids. I call it the mama bear syndrome. If you mess with our cubs, we're going to have to fight. Most of us moms already know that at some point in this quest to raise our children, we've got to put on our big-girl panties and fight.

Before you had kids, you might not have been a fighter. You could have been a go-along-to-get-along type—or perhaps a people-pleaser, easy-go-lucky, or good-girl type. Even after you had kids, you still don't really like rocking the boat or causing a fuss, despite what others may think of you. You wish you didn't have anything to fight about.

(Wouldn't life be great if everyone stayed in their lane and did their own part and minded their own business? Utopia.) But regardless of how it seems, you actually do overlook some things. You've learned, as a part of growing up, that not every battle is yours to fight. You've learned to be selective and to pick which ones need your energy.

But, mess with one of your cubs, and the passive, peaceful, ladylike being will turn into a fierce bear. It's our nature. We protect our young—and not so young. A child, the one who calls us Mama, needs our protection, especially from the enemy he can't see, but a mama bear can always sniff out when someone wants our child's blood.

Look at the moms in Chicago who boldly patrol the bloody streets—unlikely guards, but vigilant women who are just tired of the violence. Forget the picketing, forget the meetings with police and community leaders. These moms took charge—and even stopped the crime spree in one notoriously crime-ridden neighborhood. You can see it in their resolute and weary faces when they were interviewed: *We were just tired of losing our kids, of hearing the news stories. We had to do something.* These women took to the streets themselves—dressed in hot pink T-shirts with their message boldly proclaiming Mothers Against Senseless Killings (MASK). They formed their own army to combat a problem while many others just sat by and talked about the violent headlines.

For further proof that being a mama bear is a real concept, look at the mom who clears her entire kitchen—

trashes it all—from the high-powered exclusive blender to every fork and spoon. Why? Because her child has an allergic reaction to gluten—and gluten has touched all of those appliances. Expensive? Absolutely! Necessary? To this mom, protecting her child is absolutely necessary.

Or check out the mom whose child has encountered a bully. She meets with the bully's parents, talks to the teacher, has a conference with the principal—and still she switches schools. Why? Because her baby's well-being is more important than what people think of her. Driving a few extra miles to a different school is worth it to know her child won't come home in tears every day.

Oh, yeah, motherhood is not for the weak; mothers are not softies. Motherhood requires a great deal of courage and the spirit to do whatever it takes—literally, *whatever* it takes to protect our offspring. And while our mates, friends, and even other parents whisper behind our backs about our fierce roars and seemingly irrational behavior, moms have a model in the Bible.

Mama Bear Model

Look at Jochebed, often overlooked in the great story of Moses, the liberator himself. Look at the story of his birth and you will see that Moses got his spirit from his mama, straight from the bloodline. Look at Jochebed in Exodus 2, where her name really isn't even connected with her fierceness. (We know her name only from Exodus 6, in a list of genealogy that even questions if she was perhaps a later ancestor of Moses rather than his mother.) Nevertheless, the woman who birthed Moses was a mama bear, as evidenced by her story.

Moses' mom and her husband had Moses during a tumultuous time. The Israelites were in slavery, with hard and heavy labor for all. A king who knew nothing about God's promises to the people—and cared even less—had ordered all boys to be killed upon arrival. (It was literally a war on males! See Exodus 1:17.) The king needed to stop this group of people from multiplying—he didn't need any more men, no more leaders, no one trying to buck the system. He was afraid too many males meant the people, who were brutally mistreated, would be able to rise up and defeat their oppressors. They would be able to become their own army. So he said to kill the baby boys, cut them off before they would have a chance to develop and grow and become strong. But they still lived. Midwives—those charged with helping birth our little cubs—did their job well (Exodus 1:17–22). They understood their purpose was to assist moms in pushing forth their dreams, that midwives were called to help dreams come to pass, not to kill the dreams. These midwives let the Israelite babies live; they feared God. (Even in the midst of trouble, God is ever-present, regardless of how the situation looks.) The midwives didn't crush the dream upon deliverance. They let the boys live, against the order of the king. These God-fearing women were ready to be moms themselves—they already had the audacity they needed! And scripture shows God rewarded them with families (Exodus 1:21).

And when the king questioned these midwives who refused to crush the boys, they simply said: *These women are too strong; they're not like other women.* Ha! It's what women have been doing for a while. Blame it on the hormones and men will run every time. Tell them it's a "woman" thing and they won't ask any more questions. Scare them with the woman answer. It works every time— and wise moms use it when necessary.

So the king—not to be totally outwitted by the "you just don't understand women" answer—says to kill all young boys, to throw them into the Nile (Exodus 1:22). Really, kill my child? Kill the promise given to me from God, the gift, the miracle, my child? Jochebed probably fretted and cried and pondered, but she didn't give in. She didn't take the child out back and kill him herself, and she didn't just hand him over to the king to allow him to carry out his evil plan. No, somewhere, probably in the meditative moments of holding her little babe, Jochebed got an idea. Watch out when a mama bear starts to brainstorm.

She was not going to give up her child. She could see that he was special—and we know that he was—but isn't every little child we hold? Jochebed, who had already birthed Aaron and Miriam, decided to give her child away rather than risk his death. Can you see her carefully preparing a little papyrus basket and coating it with tar

(Exodus 2:3)? She cautiously places the tiny child in the basket, holding back tears and pushing forth prayers. *Sleep little baby, don't you cry. Our great God sees you. Live, don't die.* Putting him in the basket, she sets him adrift down the long Nile, turning away too soon to even see where he floats off. (Scripture says his sister, Miriam, was the one who watched the basket from a distance to see what would become of her little brother. See Exodus 2:4.) Setting baby Moses out on the river bank was better than seeing him slaughtered, cut off before his life really began. No, that mama bear would not let the king kill him. She would not let the king kill his spirit. She didn't care if everyone thought she was crazy. She was going to protect her baby. The king's edict had no power over her. I can hear Jochebed crying out loud through her actions: *My child will live. My child will not die.*

You know Jochebed, "that mom." She looks enraged, determined, feisty. Everyone may be saying, *Let it go. It will pass. It's no big deal if everyone has peanut butter sandwiches at lunch and he's allergic. He needs to build up his tolerance.* What about immunizations? Yeah, hot topic. But if you feel in your gut that this will cause danger to your special child—either getting immunized or being around others who haven't—you will be "that mom." You will forgo all the party invitations to protect your child. You will even homeschool—although you really don't want to—to protect your child! Yes, motherhood requires guts.

Hot-Button Issues

And before you judge "that mom"—as we're unfortunately prone to do in our sorority of motherhood—just think about that one issue you're ready to fight for. It might not be gluten allergies or bullies or that teacher, but there is something that will make you roar, make you come out of character and fight with every ounce of your being just to protect your special child. What will make you put your baby in a basket and send him off on the Nile?

I know I've been tempted to judge "that" mother—the one who always has an issue at the school, the one who organizes the protest, the one who writes the long, impassioned letter and posts it all over social media, the one who shows up at the playground to confront the bully, the one who pleads for no one to bring peanut butter in their lunches or to get gluten taken off the menu. But, what I've learned from "that mom" when she happens to be my friend (or when she has been me) is that this is not just a passionate issue. This is about her child's life. And when a mama bear feels her cubs are in danger, she will do anything to protect them. But just as important to note is that protecting her cub isn't a pastime for her—it takes sacrifice and real heart.

Look at Jochebed. She had a son, a child of promise and great hope. She knew he was special (Exodus 2:2), called to do something really big and great that others would be talking about for centuries upon centuries later. (Isn't it amazing how mamas just know when a child is called to greatness?!) Jochebed wanted to raise this child to be great. She wanted to bring her son into manhood, but instead she sacrificed him—to save his life. Whatever that mama bear is doing is a sacrifice. It's not easy. It's not something she takes lightly. It's not a hobby. It's not just that she likes cooking without wheat. It's to save her child's life. And it is hard, very hard. But to her, it's her only choice.

When we as mothers begin to see other mama bears doing their Jochebed-like jobs, serving their kids and protecting them, we can join in their cause when it's not even our cause. I can help save your child's life because I know I'd do whatever it takes to save mine.

My child's life is more important to me than my own. Whoa…that makes mamas even closer to God's heart. We have something in common with the Great Almighty. We would sacrifice our life to save our child's. God sacrificed Jesus' life to save ours. Can you feel that ultimate sacrifice more deeply now? It's a parent thing. I want you to live so badly that I'll do whatever it takes to give you life, and give it to you abundantly—fully and completely (See John 10:10).

We don't have the power to provide eternal life to our kids (thankfully, God's got that part covered), but we definitely can give them a better life than ours. We can try to learn more and do more. We can try to listen more and make more time. We can teach more and get more tutors. We can enroll them in every class possible to help them find their passion so they live a life filled with wonder and purpose and joy. We all just want our children to live fully.

Jochebed decided to be bold and courageous and save her son's life—or at least give him an opportunity for a different outcome. She put him in the basket and set him off. She heard about the big bad bully called Pharaoh and stood up to him the best way she knew how. Her story could have turned out differently. She could have chosen several other options. She knew the king's men were killing little boys. But that didn't stop her from giving birth to her son; she decided not to abort his potential prematurely. She pushed him through and made the ultimate sacrifice... she gave him up. Can you imagine what ran through her head as she nestled her newborn in a basket? *These Egyptians! They want to kill all of our boys. Pharaoh is out of his mind—thinking he can keep our nation down by cutting off the male line. Doesn't he know God is with us? The Almighty will make a way somehow to overcome Pharaoh's scheme. It's a part of God's plan to make us Hebrews a great nation. But as for now, I don't care what Pharaoh thinks he's doing. He's not going to kill my son. I'll die first before I see a sword come to my child's neck. No, my child will not die. He will live and I'll do whatever it takes to make that happen. If I have to give him away, I will give him a chance at life. God didn't allow me to have this special child to not fight for him to live. I'll do what it takes to increase his chance at life. Others might think I am crazy to defy Pharaoh's decree; I can't even tell my husband what I'm about to do, but I've got to give my child a chance. I just can't see him die. I can look into this baby's piercing eyes and see greatness. Death will not take my baby boy. He will live—I will make sure of it.*

Jochebed did the bold thing. She did it for her child, even as her girl child watched. Remember, our children are always watching, even more than they are listening. What message did Miriam receive that day as she saw her loving and caring mother turn into a fierce mama bear who, rather than submit to his sure death, sacrificed her son to the unknown? What spirit did Jochebed transfer to even the small Moses at the time? Was it the liberator spirit that caused him to stand up to oppression? What messages were being sent forth because Jochebed stood up and refused to take this one lying down passively?

Your Turn

What won't you do for your child? Is protecting her most important to you? How do you protect her spirit and her dreams? How do you raise him to be a warrior, to fight for what is right, to follow his passion and shine? You be that mom! The one who stands up even though everyone wants to shut you down. You will be the mom who thinks outside the box and stands guard like an army of a thousand. Why? Because your child's security and safety and growth are more important. And sometimes only you, the one who has a heart close to God's, know what is inside of your child. Sometimes only you have been given a special message, a hunch, a feeling, that your child needs to live, not die. Your child needs to do this now and you have to help, any way that you can. You are God's agent, working in collaboration with God to raise a warrior, one who will liberate many. You can't give in now. You can't give up, regardless of the sacrifice required. It's your job to push forward, Mama Bear.

You will be the mom who researches every drug they want to prescribe—you need to know, and information is unending. You will be the mom who asks for the second and third tests and fourth opinion. Why? Because you need to know. Resources may be few, but you live in a world where you can google two phrases and find a million articles. You live in a place where a tweet will get you many responses.

And most importantly, you live in a place where you can go to God and seek answers and guidance. You can hear from God through scriptures and people and messages and quiet moments about your next move. What shall I do? Where should I turn? Who can help? Ask and knock and search for the answers until you get an answer (Matthew 7:7). Jochebed had no idea how things would turn out when she sacrificed her son—but God did. Jochebed ended up getting to raise her son after all (Exodus 2:7–10). You see, Miriam had picked up her mother's bold spirit. She had stayed back and watched to see what would happen to her little brother. And when the princess (Pharaoh's daughter) set eyes on the baby liberator—Moses—her heart was opened. The princess became a mother too. And wise Miriam stepped up and asked if the princess needed someone to nurse the baby. Miriam picked up Jochebed's brave and bold spirit and ran and got her mother, the mother of the baby, to nurse her very own child. The sacrifice was worth it. Jochebed's prayers were heard. Her child would live, not die.

We as mothers are called to push forth and declare that our children will live, not die, and we'll do whatever it takes to ensure this. We won't let anyone kill our children. We won't let anyone dampen their spirits or threaten their well-being. Mamas don't give up. Mamas fight hard—and win.

Be Jochebed. Be bold. Be on guard. Protect your child with all you have. And if you need more, go get what you need.

⏤

Almighty Lord: Thank you for the gift of children and thank you for giving me your warrior spirit to protect them from whatever threatens to steal their joy or peace or well-being. Give me courage, resources, and wisdom to stand up for the welfare of my children. When I am weary, grant me strength. When I seem crazy to everyone else, provide me with the audacity to keep fighting for the sake of my offspring. Remind me to seek you each step of the way for guidance and direction. I desire love, joy, and peace for my children—for the rest of their lives. Hear my prayer. Amen.

Hannah

Successful moms always pray for their kids—from conception through adulthood.

One thing I knew before I was a mom, because I observed my own mother, is that mothers pray constantly. Moms know what 1 Thessalonians 5:17 means when it says, "Pray without ceasing" (KJV), "Never stop praying" (NLT), and "pray continually" (NIV).

Moms can take on lots of worry. After all, we are charged with caring for the souls of little ones, and not-so-little ones. We've been with our dear children all their lives—with our biological ones even before they were introduced to the world. We've felt them move and kick and hiccup inside of our wombs. We've pushed them out through pain and joyfully held them in glee and adoration and gratefulness. We've changed diaper after diaper after diaper. We've watched their teeth come in, and we've cheered them on as they walked and fell and cried. We've chosen their schools carefully. We've even tried to select their friends, just as carefully. We've wiped down restaurant seats and shopping carts before they could touch them. We've stayed up late doing projects, ironically, so they could do well in school and learn for themselves. Our children encompass a great deal of our time, our lives, and our minds. Even when they are older and away from us, we still think about them often. We wonder if they are coping. *Did he remember to...?* We moms take our jobs as caretakers very seriously and, unfortunately, that job comes with a demon called worry.

If we're wise women, we'll learn to turn all those thoughts and notes and concerns into prayers. As the old hymn says, "Oh, what peace we often forfeit, Oh, what needless pain we bear, all because we do not carry everything to God in prayer!" That hymn, "What a Friend We Have in Jesus," was sung often at the church I attended when I was growing up. I had no idea what all those words meant at the time, but when I developed a prayer life and one day literally felt so much better after praying about a situation, it clicked: God cares. When I release my every concern to God, I can live in peace and feel much lighter. The words to another one of those church songs comes to mind too: "Just a little talk with Jesus makes it right...feel a little prayer wheel turning."

Mommy, have you discovered the power of prayer? Do you know the feeling of having a prayer wheel turning?

Have you tapped into the power of praying for every little thing, every little concern about your dear child?

A Model Prayer Warrior

Enter our biblical role model, a successful mom: Hannah. She was a praying woman. She was a prayer warrior before the term even existed. I can see Hannah calling on the name of the Lord, beseeching God for a child. I see her prayer wheel turning every time I read her story in 1 Samuel 1. Notably, Hannah is the lead character in the introduction of the book that chronicles the historic rise and fall of kings in the Israelite nation. Hannah's son Samuel would go on to play a pivotal role as prophet in the unfolding drama of kings Saul and David.

But Hannah became a prayer warrior before Samuel was born. She turned to God in prayer out of necessity. She had a deep need that couldn't be filled even by her husband. When tragedy strikes your life, it can force you to your knees to cry out to God; it's one of the only benefits of tragedy, in my opinion. When life is so hard, your enemies so mean, your desires so strong, your situation so hopeless, it's time to turn to God. Hitting rock bottom can have an upside when it is the impetus for change in our prayer life. Troubles can teach us valuable lessons when we allow them to push us closer to God. And that's exactly what Hannah did.

Hannah was childless. She was barren, or as scripture says, her womb was closed (1 Samuel 1:5, NIV). The very part that we think makes us women was shut, closed, unable to produce the one thing she wanted. But Hannah knew where to turn when doors were shut. She knew whom to turn to when her tragedy struck. The deep desire for a child caused Hannah to pray as she had never prayed before (1 Samuel 1:12–14). She prayed one of those gut-wrenching cries to the Lord, the ones where your lips move but sound is barely audible. This prayer was from the soul. It was her deepest desire to have a child, and she knew only God could provide. Hannah's expressions were filled with such desire, the priest accused her of being drunk! Imagine how hard she had to be praying for someone to mistake her for a drunk woman. Hannah's prayer was deep. Hannah's prayer was sincere. Hannah's prayer was straight from her soul.

Hannah knew where to direct her request. Somehow, she knew that only God understood and only God could take care of her situation. Her husband didn't get it (1 Samuel 1:8). He repeatedly asked her why she was so distraught about her barrenness. The poor man even went so far as to remind his wife: *You have me; isn't that enough?* (Surely he didn't want her to answer him; his ego would have been crushed. Of course, she loved him, but was he enough?)

Sometimes men just don't get us. (I know, that's an understatement!) Sometimes they just don't get the position we are in as nurturers of the world. Surely Hannah's husband didn't understand the place his wife was in, sitting by watching others give birth to kids—including her husband's other wife, who was in no way understanding of Hannah's plight. The other woman (Peninnah) taunted poor Hannah because Hannah could not produce a child (1 Samuel 1:6–7). *Hey there, little Hannah. Look at my son. Look at my daughters. Aren't they pretty and smart and loving and strong? You know he won first place in the Torah bee and she recited all the books of the Pentateuch and she… My trophies are much bigger than yours—oh, you don't have any trophies, Hannah? You don't have any children to brag about and make into all the things you didn't become? Poor Hannah, you have no kids.* What senseless things we women often do to one another. We turn our gift from God into an object of envy to flaunt before some other woman, as if we are responsible for the child or children we have birthed. Really?! When we find ourselves needing to rub something in another's face, jealousy is usually at the root of our issue. Women should support, not hurt, one another. Our blessings are not meant to be taunted and dangled in front of another's face. If this is you, just stop it and check yourself internally to see why you need to do this to another woman! I think Hannah's taunter, Peninnah, was jealous of the love Hannah's husband showed to Hannah (and probably not to Peninnah). Hannah's husband gave Hannah more than he gave his other wife (1 Samuel 1:5, NIV). He loved Hannah more. And how did

Peninnah deal with this jealousy? Did she take it up with its instigator, Elkanah, the husband? No, we rarely get to the heart of the matter; instead we use people and things as pawns in a silly game. We say, *Look at what I got! Look at what my child can do! Look at how many children I'm blessed to have!* Just stop it. Don't be a Peninnah. Get to the heart of the matter, count your own blessings, confess your sins, and ask God to help you fix your jealousy issues. We don't need that junk in our lives, clouding our vision, and, dare I say, being passed along to our precious children. Pray, Peninnah. Pray like Hannah.

It's sad that Peninnah couldn't have been a better support system for her sister wife Hannah. Peninnah was in a perfect position to be more understanding of Hannah's deep desire. Many people who've never been mothers—men especially, hence, Elkanah's asking if he wasn't enough—don't quite get the bond between mother and child. There's something intrinsic in a woman that makes her heart expand when caring for a child. Many women—if not most—want to nurture a child, through parenting, mentoring, fostering, and so on. It's in us women to care, to guide, to cuddle, to love in a way that's beyond what our male counterparts can grasp. That's why sister friends, mama friends, are important in our lives. Our mates may not get us all the time. Sometimes we just need a girlfriend. And our support is special and needed in one another's lives. Peninnah missed that chance because of her jealousy.

Prayer Works

But back to the lessons dear Hannah teaches us.

Prayer is an excellent way to release our worries to our Sovereign Lord. We know that as mothers we have a lot of balls in the air. We have a good bit to be concerned about. We are charged with raising little ones—from as small as a few pounds through fully grown and in adulthood. We need to make sure our little ones' noses are clean and their vegetables are eaten and their homework is completed and their emotions are intact. We want to make sure they have friends at school and are not bullies themselves. We have to make sure they complete their applications and choose good company and look both ways when crossing the street (or driving!). Wherever our children go, a piece of us goes with them. We are always thinking of them and praying and hoping and wishing for their protection and success.

Motherhood makes you pray and motherhood changes your prayers. When was the last time you bowed and didn't include your child in your prayer? Even if we're praying for a global issue, like peace or clean water, somehow our children can become a part of that prayer. We want peace for our kids. We want to leave a better earth for our kids. We want God to protect our children—and all children, we add.

When we are blessed with motherhood, our children become the center of our prayers.

A Prayer and a Promise

Look at Hannah's prayer life. When she cried out desperately for a child, she also made a vow. Her prayer was one we call an *if, then* prayer. *If* God gave her the one thing she desired most, *then* she promised to do something. Hannah promised to give her child back. She promised to give him to the service of God—and to never cut his hair (1 Samuel 1:11). Right when she prayed, she dedicated her unborn child to the Lord. I see Hannah's faith in her tears and in her heart-wrenching prayer. She wanted to mother a child so badly that she promised to let him be God's servant, even before she saw his face. She knew that God was able to give her what she wanted, and she just wanted to show God right there how she'd act when she got what she prayed for.

Have you ever had an *if, then* prayer? What did you want so badly that you promised God something in return? What makes you negotiate with God? What makes you put your faith on the line and say you'll do something even before you see that your request has been honored? Do you follow through when that request has been granted? I'm just asking and thinking about how our prayer life serves as a model for our children. Since they are often the center of our prayers, it's good to remember to follow through on the promises we've made.

Lord, if you get us through this, I promise I will read your Word more, I will go to church more, I will give more of my time. Lord, if you get us through this, I will read to her more, I will help her with her homework more, I will be more patient, cook more vegetables, and so on. Promises, they are there. Do we follow through?

Hannah did. After she birthed her beloved son, Samuel, she brought him to the temple along with her sacrifice (as if the child weren't sacrifice enough). But Hannah honored her promise to the Lord (1 Samuel 1:24). I'm sure when she saw the beautiful child that something in her heart wanted to keep him. She wanted to coddle him and raise him and guide him and teach him the law— sometimes we hold on tighter to the things we prayed for in desperation, forgetting to honor the Giver of Life more than the gift—but Hannah remembered her promise to God. Hannah shows us how prayer really does change us. When we've spent time truly talking to God and pouring out our souls in heart-wrenching cries, we leave changed. We should leave knowing that God is the Almighty. A true encounter with God makes you leave a different person, a different mother.

Hannah could have reneged on her deal; God can show forgiveness and compassion. She could have kept her little Samuel and still raised him to honor God. But Hannah was not the same woman who wanted a child and cried out like a drunk person. She was a new woman. She had encountered God in prayer. She had received God's promise and then she had a new song of praise. Her prayer had been answered and she fulfilled her end of the deal. She gave Samuel to the Lord, and we were blessed by the work of this prophet. (See how he dealt with Saul and David, the lineage of our Savior, throughout 1 and 2 Samuel.)

In return, God gave Hannah more children. Her womb was opened and she still experienced the joy of raising and nurturing her children. And we got the blessing of Samuel. What a win-win!

Prayer Changes Us

Prayers are not just about getting our kids home safely and protecting them and looking out for them. Prayer changes us. Prayer puts us in a new position. When we encounter God, we realize that our God is real and alive and powerful and amazing. Our relationship with God grows deeper. Maybe it's because our hearts are wider and more open. Maybe it's because the role of parenthood resembles to a degree the awesome role of God's parenthood. Maybe for the first time in life we know what it is to love fully and openly and we grasp God's unbelievable love just a bit more. Whatever the reason, prayer changes moms. And we are called to share this love and faith with our children.

Let them know you are praying for them. Pray over them, out loud. Encourage them to share their prayers. When they are afraid, pray. When they are sad, pray. When they are happy, pray and thank God for answered prayers. Make prayer a part of your life, a part of your daily conversations. Pray in the car on the way to school, pray at dinnertime, pray in the middle of a fun day. Pray. Pray. Pray. It's one of the most valued gifts we can pass along to our children. And prayer is like a thank-you to God. It's modeled after Hannah's motherhood. When God gives us the gift of motherhood, it's only right to say thank you by committing to raising our children to honor and know the true Giver of Life. We have an obligation to introduce our children to the giver of "every good and perfect gift" (James 1:17, NIV).

I knew as a little girl that my mama prayed often for me. I even knew her prayers. While I cringed when she would ask God to keep me "from the wiles of the devil," I now know that my mom saw my potential—on both sides of the fence. She saw that I was impressionable and wanted to be liked and popular, which, if left unchecked, could lead down a dangerous path, the devil's wiles! But she also knew with prayer, my foundation could remain intact and I could venture down the path of perhaps helping others. Thank God for my mama's prayer (and the opportunity to share with others)! I knew she stayed on her knees often. Even as I grew older and was on my own and told her what I had done for the weekend, she said: "That's why I always have to pray for you."

She was right. I know I've gotten by on many of the prayers of my mother. It's a blessing to remember her as a prayer warrior—the exact words I said at her funeral. Don't you want your children to remember you as a prayer warrior? Not just so they can know that Mama always prayed for them, but also so they can know the power of prayer. A praying woman is powerful. A praying mama can be at peace—when the world around her is not. A praying mama can rock the cradle and influence the world. Oh, what power we women have, right in the pit of our souls, to cry out to our God and influence the world. And moms can pray honestly about their children. You can pray, just like my mother did, for God to keep me in check. Who knows a kid's issues better than Mama (when she is honest)? No need to divulge all that information to everyone, but you can take it to God in earnest prayer. Whatever it is—a short attention span, a medical need, a mean streak, a strong will—God knows how to give you peace to deal with your child. Don't tackle this job alone. It's too big for just you and your humanness. Turn your concerns into prayers. No need to forfeit any more peace or endure needless pain; we can turn to God in prayer. We have a friend waiting to hear our prayers. 1 Peter 5:7 says to throw your worries on God because he cares. I've quoted that scripture for years and found peace, but it was only recently that I connected the verse just prior to it with its powerful message. 1 Peter 5:6 (NIV) says, "Humble yourselves, therefore, under God's mighty hand, that he may lift you up in due time." It's no mistake that the very next verse says, "Cast all your anxiety on him because he cares for you."

I think humility is at the crux. If we are truly going to cast our cares upon God, we as mothers are humbly acknowledging that we don't have this caretaker-of-the-world role all figured out. We're going to have to honestly and humbly take off the superwoman cape, if only in our prayer closets, and say, "God, help!" Aren't you tired of trying to be Supermom anyway? You're already a super mom, so no need to make a compound word and make it a title, Supermom. Save the supernatural powers for God—and you get the peace. Our role and position will be so much easier when we can humbly cast our cares on the Almighty. And we can wait for God's answer, to fix the situation or to fix us. Either way, we'll get the peace and the strength and the wisdom to move forward.

Excuse me, I've got some praying to do.

God, my Heavenly Parent: Thank you for the gift of life. Thank you for the gift of children. Remind me each day to honor you and give you thanks by keeping my vows to you. Remind me to raise my children to honor you and to know you and to love you. Help me to show them what a trusting and faithful relationship with you looks like. I desire to lean and depend on you for every step of this journey. I want to walk closer and closer to you. Amen.

Abigail

Successful moms are wise examples
to their children.

Motherhood is a job God created women to do, and I
know why. God bless the single fathers out there—they
are a rare breed—but have you ever seen a man try to
multitask? My husband says it really isn't possible for
anyone to multitask. (He's no mother!) His computer-
programming background taught him you can do something called time slice but not actually do two things at a
time. He's convinced it may appear that you're multitasking, but *time slicing* means you're still doing one before
the other and probably giving one more attention than the
other. Women, and particularly moms from all four cor-
ners of the earth, know that nothing would get done if we
focused on one thing at a time. A mom has to be able to
check homework, cook dinner, talk on the phone (y'all still
do that? Motherhood's turned me into a text-only type

of girl!), check e-mail, pay a bill, console a wounded one, and hold it all together. Whew...I'm tired just typing that and thinking about all we do in one single day. Men don't understand us. And that's okay; we don't understand them a lot of the time either.

To further prove how single-task-oriented our male counterparts are, the only time my husband has done laundry is when I was recovering from my C-section, prior to my sister's arriving from out of town. He was out of underwear, so it was an emergency. He woke up that morning in a panic, knowing he had "so much to do." When he gathered the one load of clothes to be put into the washer, he huffed and puffed. When he finally got all the items in the washer, he felt accomplished. And you know what he did? He sat down! He sat right by my bedside and proclaimed, "I got those clothes in the washer, but I still have so much to do."

No joking, moms! My husband thought waiting for the clothes to complete the rinse cycle was work; he didn't see this thirty-five-minute time frame as the opportunity to complete anything else. Nope. But I didn't give him too hard of a time. (My daughter's now six and I'm still talking about it! Oh for the luxury to wait on the rinse cycle.)

Men are just configured differently. They do things differently, process things differently, react differently, have different priorities. It's not wrong (mostly); it's just men.

Successful moms need to study their man and know

what works and doesn't work. It's not manipulative...it's wise and smart.

Abigail, Wisdom at Work

Enter one of my favorite women of the Bible: the wise, discerning, and intelligent Abigail. You may or may not have heard of her—she's just that little known—but once you learn more of her story, trust me, she may just be your favorite mom too. Her story is primarily found in 1 Samuel 25, and again she's a woman used to play an important role to make way for the great King David, whose lineage leads to Jesus. Can't you see how valuable women were? And still are! Humans may lift up patriarchs of the Bible, but the matriarchs' stories are still present and alive and speaking to us today.

My fave girl Abigail was the wife of Nabal. The Bible says flat out that his name meant *fool*—and he acted accordingly (1 Samuel 25:25). We can only imagine what this woman put up with as the mate of a fool. Moms often have to look out for their children *and* their mates. For the good of the family, Mom is often the fixer. She is the one who has studied the world and the way things work; whether good or bad, fair or unfair, Mom understands. She's studied the system and the teachers and the friends. Mom knows. She's always on the lookout for the good and bad and nondescript. Let's look closer at how Abigail handled the good and the bad.

Abigail's husband, Nabal, is literally described in scripture as "surly and mean in his dealings" (1 Samuel 25:3, NIV). He was a no-good businessman who had a great deal of property and was considered very wealthy. He was not pleasant to deal with—and apparently his wise wife had studied him enough to know this about him. When David ventured near Nabal's territory, David sent word to Nabal. He wished good health on his household. David's messengers also reminded Nabal how well David's men had treated his men. In essence, David was saying, *We did you a favor; would you be so kind as to return that favor and care for us while we are near you?* Helping David and his men out wouldn't have been a problem for Nabal.

But because he was "surly and mean," Nabal refused. Instead, he even questioned who David was. He said many servants had been breaking away and David could have been just a runaway servant. I doubt Nabal knew nothing of David because David was well known; songs were sung about him (1 Samuel 18:7). But, Nabal's "intelligent and beautiful" (yep, exactly what scripture calls her in 1 Samuel 25:3, NIV) wife, Abigail, knew about David, as is demonstrated by what happens next.

You see, that wise woman was on the lookout. She may have been quietly working behind the scenes, tending to her work, but she heard what Nabal had done. She had evidently garnered trust from her servants—as all wise women do—and one told her what had just happened. Even the servants knew this was the wrong move for Nabal, and the servant knew whom to go to to try to get this wrong righted. Wise, discerning women are known throughout the land—in the schools, community, church, home. We don't have to broadcast our wisdom (the wise never do) or gain the spotlight for our heroic acts; people just know. People know whom they can trust; people know whom to call when they need a faithful mom; people just know.

Abigail's servants knew to report to the wise woman of the household and tell her what the foolish Nabal had just done. When Abigail heard the story, she didn't need any interpretation. She didn't need to consult with her friends or plead with her foolish husband to change his mind. This wise woman knew exactly what to do and she did it quickly (1 Samuel 25:18). She realized that Nabal had just turned down the man who would be the next king of Israel. She knew that this was a tumultuous time for David and his people. They had just buried the beloved Samuel (1 Samuel 25:1). Abigail knew the temperature and climate of the world around her—as wise and discerning women do. She knew about David's acts and how kind he had been to Saul and even to foolish Nabal.

She did what a wise woman does when she knows something. She quickly worked behind the scenes. Abigail got together lots of provisions for David's men. She instructed her servants to move quickly and carry the loads to David and his men. She was behind them. No one mentioned this to Nabal. (No wonder!)

When Abigail saw David, she assumed a humble position. She bowed down and apologized for Nabal's actions. She took the blame for her husband's foolishness. She told David she hadn't seen or heard about his request until Nabal had turned him down. She came to make up for what her husband had done.

She also appealed to David's sense of right. She told him that God had used her to stop him from getting blood on his own hands; surely, David would have had Nabal killed for this major act of disrespect, but Abigail prevented that. The wise woman kept the future king free from blood guilt, and she made sure he and his troops had plenty to eat and drink. She took care of it. She fixed things.

Mamas Know

Wise mamas know when to act. Wise mamas know whom to talk to. If we don't, we wait and we watch. We pray often for God's guidance. We're not always out in front, but we do know what's going on. We don't usually miss a beat because we have our eyes and ears open at all times. And when action is required, we know how to respond in humility and with purpose. I love how Abigail went straight to the source. She didn't worry about how it would look or about protocol at the time. She was smart enough to know that David shouldn't have blood on his hands, and she used that information, along with the gifts she brought, to calm him down and make him come to his senses. She knew her husband was a fool, but she didn't let that bring harm to her household. She protected her family in spite of her husband's foolishness.

You've got to know whom you're dealing with. You've got to know your mate's strengths as well as his weaknesses. It's not our job to fix those weaknesses either. It's our job to stay tuned to God and God's promptings. It's our job to stay tuned to the happenings around our family and act when necessary. Not every problem needs to be fixed by us, but when one does, we know what to do. We can push pride down and humbly get to the heart of the matter. It's not about us or even our mates; it's really about saving and protecting our family.

Acting like Abigail can be scary. What if we're wrong? What if we get caught? What if things don't quite turn out the way we need them to? That's where faith comes in. Abigail did what she knew was right—and she did it quickly. She let God do the rest. Don't you think she wondered why she was caught up with such a foolish and mean man? Don't you think life was hard for her? I don't know what Nabal did to her or how he treated her, but given that his name—his being—was foolish, I imagine he wasn't the perfect husband. But Abigail was smart and didn't make her move too soon. She watched and waited and, most importantly, she did the right thing for her family.

. . .

I've heard stories of wise women who escape abuse because of their children. They've risked their lives and secured housing for their children because they didn't want them to grow up watching abuse. They might have stayed otherwise, but, for their children, they sought better. Every woman should live in a violence-free environment—for her sake and for her kids' sake. But it takes a strong, smart woman to leave craziness for the unknown. It takes faith to leave a level of belonging—as dysfunctional as it may be—for the unknown. It also takes faith to confront the craziness we do know, inside or outside our homes: the rules that make no sense, the coach who won't let up, the bully and her parents, who are as ruthless as she is.

Abigail teaches us that we can be discerning and wise when dealing with the crazy fools in our lives. We can stay watchful and prayerful and await the right moment to launch a crusade. We don't have to publicize our efforts; we just need to move wisely and stealthily like Abigail. We may never get the credit or be seen as the smart one moving behind the scenes, but we get the job done. We act on behalf of our families, and we make the best decisions for them. We think of others and how our actions will impact them. We're wise and intelligent, and, dare I say, beautiful, just like Abigail. After all, pretty is as pretty does.

Abigail may appear as the cleanup woman in Nabal's crazy world; she may seem like the one saving his hide time and time again. She may seem so undeserving of the treatment she probably receives from Nabal, but in the end—as always—good rules. Without any help at all from Abigail, Nabal falls dead (1 Samuel 25:38). And when David hears about the fool's death, the future king wastes no time swooping up the beautiful and intelligent and now-widowed Abigail (1 Samuel 25:40). Now, Abigail might be moving from crazy to more crazy, given how David's household turns out, but there's no doubt, sister Abigail can handle all the mess that comes with being royalty. She was prepped and primed very well.

I know life seems unfair at times. You may feel you're always the mom making sense of everything. You're the one called in to clean up the messes left by your mate, your kids, others. But use Abigail's wisdom and intelligence as a model, and patiently and humbly await your reward from a King who's much wiser than Nabal and David!

God sees all. God knows all. And at just the right time, God gives us what we need, whether that's a helping hand from a neighbor or the wisdom to step out on a path not ventured before. If we rely on God for wisdom, God will grant it (James 1:5). And we can be like Abigail, a beacon of wisdom in the midst of craziness. Our children need to see wise behavior and not just craziness. David's sons reaped the consequences of some of their father's missteps—Amnon raped his sister (2 Samuel 13); Absalom sought revenge by killing his brother and trying to overthrow his father (2 Samuel 13, 18). Blood was everywhere and peace remained ungrasped in this family, but never once is anything negative recorded about Abigail's children, Kileab and Daniel (who are mentioned only in 2 Samuel 3:3 and 1 Chronicles 3:1, respectively). Abigail's kids apparently stayed under the radar and out of the family drama; they were wise men. I think their mother's wisdom and experience showed them how to live in a sea of craziness and dysfunction. David and his household may have had lots of drama, but somehow Abigail kept her children untouched by it all. Mom, you may not be able to stop the craziness in this world and even in your own family, but you *can* show and teach your kids how to live wisely among it.

I can hear Abigail's bedtime stories and drive-time talks, dispensing her wisdom to her children: *You don't have to get involved, honey; it will work itself out. Just sit and wait, you'll get your chance. Watch, wait, and listen—your time will come. You don't have to be crazy to beat crazy. Be wise. Be godly. Godly always wins. Just wait and see. I'm a living witness. God will take care of you. God will fight your battles. Watch and see.*

—

Dear God: Give me the wisdom of Abigail. Give me discernment to know when to act and when to wait. Teach me to wait for you before I make any move to protect my family. I know you see the crazy in this world; teach me to lead by example as I show my children how to navigate this world according to your standards. Remind us all that love does overcome evil—regardless of how things look now. I want to trust you and believe you and watch all things work together for good. Amen.

Sarah

Successful moms balance faith in God
and action.

Moms of thriving children are usually all about action.
Such moms don't just sit around passively waiting for
things to get done. If something needs to be done, Mom
will do it. The house needs cleaning; we get it done.
Dinner needs cooking; we do it. Schedules need to be
arranged; we open up Outlook or break out the old wall
calendar and begin color-coding our days or setting up
carpool assignments. When volunteers are needed at the
school, call moms. We get the job done. We're a lot like
Sarah in the Bible. I love Sarah. I love Sarah's story. She's
one of the women of the Bible we often refer to when we
think of women having kids in old age. She's like Elizabeth. They both bore kids well after the normal time of
child-bearing. Hannah may have been without child for
a while, but she wasn't seen as being old; her baby was

just delayed. Even Rachel, who cried to the Lord for a child, wasn't described as old, just barren. Her womb was opened when she was still young and apparently of child-bearing age.

But Sarah was ninety, and her husband was one hundred when she gave birth to their promised child, Isaac (Genesis 17:17). And that's one of the reasons I love Sarah and her story; it once again demonstrates a major theme throughout scripture and life: God does just what God promises. Even after so many years, God's commitment did not have an expiration date on it. And that's good news for moms everywhere. We can sometimes be so wrapped up in the joys and pains of raising our kids and tending to our families that we may forget about our own personal dreams or goals—or the promises we feel we heard from God. Does life stop with motherhood? Does life end with me always caring for another? I don't think so. While motherhood is a huge part of a woman's life, it isn't all the pieces of the puzzle. If you have been made a promise, it can be fulfilled in due time. You may be the last one to the party, but you can still go to the party and have a great time. Sarah showed up to motherhood late, but she still showed up. God still delivered on the promise. Sarah had her promised child, Isaac.

You, a mother already, may show up late to the other parties, but you can still attend. Don't let motherhood—or any season of your life—force you to give up any other dreams. You may need to wait and wait and prepare now, but you don't have to give up on your dreams. Dreams can come true at any age. Keep believing and dreaming.

But Sarah's late arrival to the mommyhood party is not my only reason for loving her story. You see, despite what others may say about Sarah, I believe she was truly a woman of faith. Earlier in her story, in Genesis 15, God had promised to make Abraham (Abram) into a great nation. God would establish his people from the line of Abraham. So yeah, Abraham thought it and even said it to God: *I don't have an heir. How can I have a nation if I don't even have a child to bear my name and reproduce and make a nation? Come on, God.* (Isn't it ironic and funny how we think God hasn't thought about these things?) Well, God does answer Abram and lets him know that Abram will have a child from his own body to call his heir (Genesis 15:4). Abram had thought perhaps his servant would be his heir (Genesis 15:3). Sarah (at that time called Sarai) thought she understood this promise. She hadn't been able to bear a child, so she thought she'd carry out the promise of God. She believed that her husband would be the father of a child (as God had explicitly said), so she made an arrangement for him to be a daddy. Sarai took action and gave her servant, Hagar, to Abram to produce a child. Huh?

Yep, Sarah hooked Abraham up with Hagar so they could have a child—and they did (Ishmael). When I used to hear this story, everyone blamed Sarah. She was using her servant, Hagar, to get a child, and then—as human nature would have it—she turned on the woman she set up (Genesis 16:6)! (Sarah! Girl, what were you thinking? That was never going to work!) Many people identify with Hagar, the poor servant who probably didn't have a choice in the matter. And I get that. I do. She was a pawn in her master and mistress's game, a sad plot repeated often in history's playbook. I don't want to take away from Hagar's plight.

But let's look at Sarah just a little closer. Sarah was faith-filled. She believed God! She literally believed that God would give Abram a son through his own body (as stated in Genesis 15:4). She interpreted that to mean that maybe the son wouldn't be from her own body, and if that was so, she was not going to stand in the way. She was going to help the plan along—and perhaps that's where she got into some trouble. She believed God's Word, but she also thought she had to help it along. She was the person you'd go to when you needed something done, much like us moms. She was the woman who could get the job done, regardless of the obstacles and challenges. Sarah would be the woman I'd want on my committee. She'd get it done. Yes, Sarah believed God...she literally believed that he'd do what he said: give Abraham an heir through his own body. And because she believed, she put her faith in action and started to make things happen. Sarah was used to getting it done. Can't you hear her rattling the dishes, moving the furniture, and making room for the promises of God? Her honey-do list was long and left no room for interpretation. She spelled it out even for Abraham. *This is what you are to do; don't add to it or take away from my well-thought-out plan; this is how we will get exactly what God promised. You know God said you would have an heir to build a mighty nation upon, right? Well, you're not getting any younger—and neither am I. We've got to get moving with God's promises and plan. So take Hagar, my lovely young maid. Sleep with her—but just once! Don't get used to it. We're doing this only so she can give us that heir we need. I'll make sure she's ready to have a child and keeps her body nice and healthy—after all, she'll be carrying the promised child. So get ready. Sleep with her when I tell you to—and only when I say so, Abe. This will work out. You just watch and see. God made us a promise and I know God is faithful. So you do exactly what I say when I say it and everything will work out just fine. Got it, honey?*

Helping God Along

Isn't that the conundrum we moms often find ourselves in? *I believe the promises of God. Now let me help them along.* And I know why it's a conundrum. We are women of action. We want to work things out. We want to push God's hand. If God promised it, we believe and we are ready for action. We are ready to see the manifestation of the promised plan. It's going to happen; let's just make it happen. Why wait around?

But, Mommy, you know it's a balancing act. We have to walk that tightrope carefully, prayerfully, seeking God each step of the way. *You told me my child would do this; I believe my child can do this. I want to push and push and push.* But sometimes, the true faith comes in waiting and watching God's plan unfold, even when we're not sure how it will.

I like Sarah. She may be talked about for forcing things and creating a big mess (You think you have family drama? Try blending a love child into the mix when Mama works for the wife!), and it didn't turn out well for Sarah and Hagar, at least not at first; but God has a miraculous way of cleaning up our mess and creating beauty. And even while cleaning up our mess, God remains God. God's plans didn't change because of Sarah's bold faith and her pushy ways. God took care of Hagar and Ishmael (and made them some promises too—see Genesis 21:18), but God remained true to the plan at hand. Look here, Sarah; God's got this. I see your faith. I see that you believe God will give Abe a descendant to build that great nation, but, girl, step out of the way. God's got this. Watch God work.

And isn't that the message we moms need to remind ourselves of all the time? God's got this. God sees our children—better than we do. God knows our situation much more clearly than we do. I know we moms are often tempted to move in and change things for our precious children; after all, it's a promise from God (right?!). Your craftiness and quick mommy action, which is akin to a superhero's, can fix it. We can be Olivia Pope and clean up the mess for our child. But what if God has a plan that doesn't involve Mom's fixing everything for her child or children? What if the real lesson will be learned in the waiting moment? What character can be built in our child if we refuse to pick up the phone and arrange the next job interview, the next event? What if… what if we waited and let our children step things up? How would their faith in God be deepened if they had to pray and pray and wait and wait? How much more would they learn the value of being a self-starter and taking initiative? What better way to learn than having to actually do a few things for themselves—without Mom waiting to fix every little mishap or change the entire course?

My sister told her eleven-year-old son to turn in his extra-credit work a few days before grades for the semester were due. My nephew, in his confidence, told her he was certain he was doing great in his classes and he didn't need the extra credit. She acknowledged his confidence and then told him to turn the work in anyway, just to make sure. But he didn't turn it in. Well, imagine the lesson he learned when his grades came in: he had all A's and one B. Yep, that B could have been an A if he had turned in the extra-credit work—just as his mom had advised. (It's a universal kid law that they always know better than Mom!) My sister was tempted to call the teacher—after all, the work was done and probably sitting in his backpack. But she decided not to. She pushed past her desire to brag about her son's 4.0 grade point average; she pushed past the need to fix a simple problem with a phone call or e-mail to the teacher. That day, she decided not to be the fix-it mom. The lessons my nephew learned that day—it makes sense to follow through; it can't hurt to be certain; go ahead, take one more step—will be lessons my sister probably will never ever have to teach him again. He's learned them. He's seen them in action. Tough situation; great lesson learned!

Helicopter Mama

I know it is popular to fly your helicopter just above your child's head and make sure he has everything done just right and on time. I know Tiger Moms are getting credit for pushing their children the extra mile and raising them in a countercultural fashion. I get it. I'm tempted too. *She's only five; I can fix this*—this time. But what happens to a generation that is used to having Mommy fix it? Ask your co-workers. Ask anyone working in a field with millennials today, even if that is you yourself. Some, not all, young adults haven't figured out how life works. They've been so used to having Mommy fix it and swoop in like Sarah and try to push God's hand that we've created a big mess. We have twenty-year-olds not knowing how to do laundry in dorms. We have young people not being able to negotiate their way out of a fight—because Mommy stopped the bullying. We have grown people not knowing how to pick themselves up when they fall—because they were always caught. We have a brood of privileged children expecting the world to treat them with as much privilege as Mom does. I once read that it's important to teach your kids they are special...and then to tell them as young adults that they really aren't any different from anyone else. It's not about self-esteem; it's about breaking the cycle of entitlement: *You are a great kid and you can do anything and you are the best, but so is everyone else in this world—regardless of what stage they seem to be in right now. You can't expect special treatment just because your mama thinks you're special.* Everyone's mama thinks that (or she should). Our children's response should be to be their best while respecting and caring for others as well.

It's a balancing act. Lord knows we want to help our children reach their full potential. We feel it's a promise from God. And it probably is. I know God can share things with mothers during those precious wee hours when we are half-sleepy and half-tired but still exhilarated because of the tiny mouths we get to feed. We "get" to do this motherhood thing. We "get" to raise a generation. We "get" to be called Mommy. And we can sometimes think that means we have to fix things. We have to make God's promises come to pass. News flash: As much as our kids and families need us, God can be God alone. God can bring about all those promises without our pushing and prodding and manipulating and trying to force things to come to pass.

Along with the lesson of helping herself and becoming independent, I want my child to see Mommy waiting for God. I want my child to hear me praying the promises of God over her and waiting for them to come to pass. I don't want her to see me forcing something that isn't the will or timing of God. I want her to see that my trust and faith in God is such that I can wait because I believe God.

But what do you do when you're tempted like Sarah to fix it every time? I think it starts with your view of your role as Mom. While your family may think you are the fixer, it's important to know that you really are not. Point your children to Christ. Have them learn to pray and wait for God for some things. Seek balance in your own life, so your kids will not become your everything, which will entice you even more to make their little worlds perfect. You're not doing them a favor; one day, they will find out that life just isn't perfect. It is filled with ups and downs, good and bad. Some circumstances just don't turn out the way we want them to. It's better for your kids to learn to deal with disappointment at a young age with you by their side, with a faithful and encouraging word, rather than learning to deal with it as an adult. Perhaps as adults, when disappointment strikes, they will recall your example and your encouragement.

When mothers have balance, they are not clouded by the sweetness and tenderness of their children. We are less likely to hover too closely to our kids when we have our own lives going on, whether it's a hobby (try your best not to break a date with yourself, no matter the interruption), a healthy relationship with our mate (date night is for you—and try not to fill the conversation with discussion about the kids; you have something else to talk about, don't you?), girlfriends (don't you miss them? Try, try, try to schedule a date out with them and don't cancel it.). Work on your dreams, those things you may have put on hold while becoming Mom. Maybe you're preparing through education or a workshop or reading a book or volunteering in a position that gives you close-up experience in your dream role.

Sarah was all-consumed with God's promise to build a great nation from Abraham. Perhaps had she been working on some other aspects of her life, she wouldn't have felt the need to push God's hand. She could have relaxed and waited with anticipation. Who knew she'd be ninety with a baby?! We moms would tell her now not to waste her time prodding and pulling and trying to make things happen. When she was blessed with Isaac, she had her hands full. Oh what priceless time she gave up trying to play God.

Whatever space and time and phase you find yourself in today, Mommy: let your faith prompt you to wait for God for his promises to come to pass. And while you're waiting, do something to enjoy yourself. Do something that doesn't involve obsessing over your child or his scores or her talents. Our kids are watching—and they deserve to see a balanced mom filled with faith—watching and waiting for the promises of God to come to pass.

~

Faithful God: You know my heart and you know my desire to make everything just right for my children. I want the very best for each of them. But I need your help. I need you to show me how to balance my faith and trust in you with my actions. I know you know exactly what my children need and exactly what I need. Give me the faith to truly wait for you to fulfill your promises. Grant me the wisdom to know when to move, how to walk according to your will and your plans, and when to be still and wait. Use my life to show my children the beauty of balancing faith and works. Amen.

Elizabeth

Successful moms believe the impossible—
no matter how long it takes.

If we're honest, even as successful moms, we'd have to say that: waiting for God is not easy. It can sometimes feel downright impossible to wait and wait and wait for something we've prayed for and sought God for. Fertility can be like that. We have more and more fertility options available to us, yet many women still face major challenges when waiting for their bundles of joy. We don't know if we can or cannot have children until we try to have a child—and for many, like me, that can happen well after the biologically optimal years.

We, unlike our successful role models in the Bible, don't get hooked up with our husbands at the tender age of thirteen or fourteen (thank God), when our bodies are young and ready to bear children. Many of us are not mentally, emotionally, or spiritually mature like our bodies until much later. And since motherhood is one of the biggest sacrifices in life, it makes psychological sense to wait until we're older and ready for kids.

But what happens when you've waited and waited for your husband and right mate to have children and then you try and try and try? While this is not my story per se, I know many women—especially now that we are delaying childbirth intentionally to pursue higher education, careers, and sometimes just life—who say they waited only to find out something wasn't functioning properly or they just couldn't get pregnant. I'm thankful for the fertility options for these women, but even those great options can bring about a good deal of shame and frustration, not to mention fiscal burden. Some women simply cannot afford the cost of trying to get assistance for what we thought would happen naturally. Where is God in all of these circumstances? Can you imagine how it feels to look around you and see women of all ages, nationalities, economic situations, and marital statuses producing babies— some almost effortlessly—and you and your mate cannot produce one? Or, you can't carry one to term?

What happens to this woman? What happens to a dream deferred—the thoughts of carrying a child and bringing him home from the hospital and showing him to all your friends? What happens when you've created a nursery for your little one and it remains empty? How does faith carry you then?

Or what happens when your blessing comes along with special needs and demands much more from you than you ever imagined she would? Sure, you knew (or thought you knew) that having a child would require his total dependence on you for a few years, but what happens when you find out your child will always be dependent on you for even the simplest of tasks—seeing, walking, getting dressed, eating? Parents of special-needs children didn't sign up for a child who needed constant care, but still they somehow find the strength and wisdom to carry on. Their lives are changed in more ways than one.

When our dreams are deferred—or show up looking like a bad dream—bitterness can easily set in. *Why me?* can be our chorus, the line we repeat over and over—if only in our hearts. *Why did this happen to me? Why can't things go the way I've planned them?* All are versions of the same tune, and they can lead to bitterness and resentment. Bitterness is the result of years of disappointment. Bitterness can almost be a fence, a guard, wrapped around our hearts to protect us from hoping and dreaming again. Many of us women find ourselves keeping company with bitterness—especially after we've lived a few years, working on our dreams, waiting for our dreams, and what has shown up, Lord knows, is not what we expected. Or we're somehow left still wanting and still waiting for what we thought was a given, or for what was indeed promised to us. Even though we may try not to—because we know better—we still think this life thing and this faith thing should follow a certain formula. Trust, believe, pray, and voilà, we have our answers and the promises of God. But the reality is that we trust, believe, pray, and wait and wait and wait. So, in an effort to not return to that longing place of hoping and desiring, we allow bitterness to be our constant companion. We may cover it with a smile—or we may not—but it usually seeps through in our conversations, attitudes, and actions. Is there redemption for the bitter, disappointed soul?

Elizabeth, an Alternative to Bitterness

I introduce Elizabeth. Her story is found in the first chapter of Luke, where this writer of the gospel gives particular attention to the plight of women (which makes it my favorite gospel, the one I turn to first when I want to read about Jesus' life and hear from the women who contributed to his story). Elizabeth is a woman who perhaps was bitter—or could have easily been a candidate to build a solid fence of bitterness around her heart. Elizabeth was a classic good girl. Luke 1:6 describes her as "righteous." She and her husband lived carefully following the law before God. They obeyed all the rules. Yet, this holy and righteous couple, who were now well along in years, did not have any children. The good-girl, rule-follower Elizabeth was barren. She had not been given the gift of childbirth, which was seen as a mark of womanhood then much more than it is today. But, either Elizabeth was redeemed from the bitterness caused by missed appointments and disappointment or she was blessed enough to be protected from bitterness; either way, she teaches us how to live this life, even in the midst of disappointment.

Elizabeth was married to Zechariah, a righteous priest. The couple did what they were supposed to do; they followed God's commands—they both even came from priestly lines. They were, in essence, the favored children. Elizabeth met the right man and did the right thing, but still her womb was empty. Doesn't disappointment hit us harder when we think we've done all we were supposed to do? We waited for our mates, we changed our ways, we prayed, we went to church, we helped the old lady down the street (and on and on and on). And even if we didn't do all that was right, is *this* our punishment? What happened to the God of mercy and forgiveness and compassion? *Surely, God gave her (my neighbor, friend, sister) her heart's desire and she's no holier than I am. I know her story,* you say to yourself, too ashamed to make the words audible. Surely, this isn't fair.

I don't know if Elizabeth said these things, although she probably had cause to. In her time, bearing a child had a more significant impact on a woman's life than it does now. And she didn't have fertility treatment centers or adoption agencies to turn to. She had her longing, her desires, her prayers, and her righteousness to hang on to.

Elizabeth may even have stopped praying for a child. When you've gone a long time with unanswered prayers, it is easy to stop praying. While the hole remains, you sometimes forget to ask God for help. You stop. *It's been too long; this situation will not change so I better go ahead and learn to live with it (or build a fence around my hopes to stop them from growing and reaching and extending).* When you've longed for an answer to prayer for an extended amount of time, you can sometimes learn to resist hope. It feels safer that way. You can learn to erase the request from your prayer list—never truly from your heart or soul—but you don't verbalize the desire anymore. It's better to keep it quietly tucked away internally. Maybe no one will realize you never got your request or they might just figure this is the way you like your life.

Finally, Answered Prayer

But one day, long after she had constantly beseeched God for her child, Elizabeth's prayer was answered. Can you imagine how Elizabeth felt? Can you imagine what ran through her mind? Joy, unbelief, fear, shame (*What will people say: I'm an old woman having a child?!*), even anger:

(*Why now, Lord?! Will I be able to raise a child in my old age? Will I be able to deliver this child without dying?!*).

I can hear Elizabeth's cries of uncertainty, tainted with gratefulness and perhaps even disbelief. *Now, Lord? You say we're finally going to have a child? Aren't we too old for this? I know about Sarah and Abraham, but does that really still happen? What am I to do? What do you expect from me—since you've finally answered my prayer? It's been so long since I even petitioned you for a child—I thought you hadn't heard or had decided Zechariah and I were better off without children. I had learned to love my nieces and nephews as my own. I had learned to suppress my desire to be called Mama. And now, out of the blue, you place a child in my womb? I don't know quite what to make of all this. I tried talking to Zechariah, but he can't say a word, poor thing. I guess you gave him some revelation that day in the temple. He hasn't spoken since then. But he seems okay with the news that we're having a baby. I just hope this goes okay. I'd hate to get my hopes up and then have them crushed. God, I guess I'm going to have to trust you on this one too.*

Years and years had gone by and she had not had a child. Now, in her old age, she was pregnant. Elizabeth remained in seclusion for five months (Luke 1:24). But in the midst of her seclusion, Elizabeth received a visitor, and how she reacted tells me this woman was indeed a role model. Elizabeth got a visit from Mary, who had just found out she was pregnant with the Savior of the world. Mary was much younger than Elizabeth and just engaged to be married. I still get chills reading how Elizabeth greeted Mary in Luke 1:42. Think about it: Elizabeth was well up in age, dealing with this life-changing, faith-altering being growing in her womb—late, but still there. She had been dealing, I'm sure, her entire adult life with the concept of a dreamed deferred, a prayer unanswered, and now it was answered and she was still trying to wrap her mind around a miracle (as if that could ever really happen) and in came a bouncing, young pregnant girl who wasn't even married. Jealousy could easily have set in. *How can she get pregnant so easily—without even knowing a man! Likely story, little Mary.* Or *I had to wait so long for my dream to come true; what makes her so much better than me? Why does she have the charmed life and mine is filled with waiting?* These and so many other questions could have been thrown at Mary, but instead, Elizabeth had another response.

Elizabeth's unborn babe leaped inside of her as she greeted the mother of Jesus! Elizabeth affirmed that Mary was carrying the Savior. The child inside of Elizabeth confirmed that Mary was the mother of Christ. Elizabeth rejoiced as if another prayer had been answered, that she had met the Savior and the vessel God had chosen to deliver him to the world. Elizabeth did have a question for her relative Mary: "Why am I so favored, that the mother of my Lord should come to me?" (Luke 1:43). Oh sweet Elizabeth! Bitterness did not reside with her, but humility did. She was actually humbled in the presence of Mary, who was carrying the Savior. Elizabeth knew the real deal when she saw and felt it. She rejoiced with Mary for all that God was doing in her life.

Not only was Elizabeth allowed to carry forth a child who would get others ready for the Savior (a blessing in and of itself), but she was able to meet the Savior, the one who would change the world and right the wrong. *Oh my, what have I done to deserve such a visit? What have I done to be granted my petition?* This woman's questions turned from *Why haven't I had a child?* to *Oh my, why am I favored?*

When we encounter Christ in a real and authentic fashion, we can't help but be humbled and ask why we are favored, regardless of our current situation. When we encounter Christ, we can't help but rejoice with others; it's what we're called to do (see Romans 12:15). One of the keys to releasing bitterness is to allow God's transforming power to help you see good in others—and to rejoice with them, regardless of what is going on in your life. You never know when your time for rejoicing will come, so you might as well get some practice in.

In a Moment

Life can change in an instant. We can move from being disappointed to pleased in a second. We can move from no child to a houseful in what feels like seconds. We can go from nursing a baby to an empty nest in what feels like seconds. While the days are long as we're raising kids, the years are short. And what felt like work turns into questions of *Where did the time go?*

As we meet disappointments—and there are many on the motherhood journey—may we keep the spirit and attitude and story of Elizabeth in mind. It can all change so quickly. In a second we can go from being empty to being full, from wondering, *Why not me, Lord?* to asking, *Why me, Lord?* The weeping is at night—and that always seems longer—because we're sleeping and resting. But day comes; morning comes, and it can bring joy and hope and new life.

Don't let the fence of bitterness keep you from hoping and dreaming and working and serving and praying. Keep asking God for what you want and need. Keep hoping for a breakthrough, an answer, and the help you need. As the old folks in my Baptist church used to say: God may not come when you want him to, but he's always right on time.

We don't have the eternal calendar so it's hard for us to understand what "right on time" means. It feels it should be now (all the time), but it's not. God sees us. God hears us. God knows us and God knows what time it is! In Elizabeth's case, she had a great calling, an assignment that was bigger than her biological clock; it was greater than her own personal calendar. God had chosen Elizabeth and Zechariah to birth the predecessor to Christ. We call Elizabeth's child, John the Baptist, the forerunner to Jesus. It was a timing issue. God needed some things to be in place before the Savior was introduced to the world. Therefore, God needed some things to be in place before the forerunner came. John was born six months ahead of Jesus—his assignment was to set the stage and to share with the people that someone great was on the way. Elizabeth couldn't have had John any earlier than she did. He was right on time to fulfill his God-ordained mission.

Oh, if we could view our delays and disappointments with heavenly visions we'd see they were not late but were really right on time. If we could avoid comparing our timetables to our neighbor's timetables, we'd understand that our journeys were uniquely designed for us, matching our strengths, weaknesses, and experiences. Isn't it ironic how we mothers often try to rush our kids to sit up, walk, wear pull-ups and real underwear, read, and learn to play the piano? It's as if we were on the sidelines coaching them and pushing them and prodding them to grow faster and faster so we could sit back and say how quickly the time went and bemoan that we didn't cherish the days more. Waiting for our dreams and answers to prayers can also be compared to eager mothers on the sidelines. We wish and pray and base our hopes on the day this will happen. We dream and fantasize about the day. We wait and wait and wait, often not realizing how our character and other qualities are being developed during the waiting period. And then—after we've just about given up on that prayer—we look up and the very thing we desired has happened. He's reading on his own. She's caring for herself. She is getting along with others. He has come out of his shell. Live in the moment and enjoy whatever stage you (or your child) may be in. Find the joy in this moment as a mother and as a woman. You're developing some character—you wouldn't want bitterness to keep you from learning the lessons and enjoying this day.

I want to live like Elizabeth—open to the possibilities of God. I want to be known as a righteous woman who prayed and sought God for everything. I want to follow God no matter what time it is. I want to guard my heart against bitterness when life disappoints me. I want to guard my heart against hopelessness when it seems there is no answer. I want to forever hope and trust in God's calendar and God's timing—even when I don't understand it or can't figure it out. I want to rejoice and weep when my sister rejoices and weeps. I want to praise God for other people's answered prayers, because I know my answers have got to be on their way. Why? Because I serve a big God and I still wait and hope for God to blow my mind and answer my prayers in ways I can't ask or imagine (Ephesians 3:20).

That's the key to avoiding bitterness while waiting, like Elizabeth!

Holy One: Give me the patience and wisdom to wait for you to answer my every prayer. I also seek your help in guiding me to enjoy each moment of the motherhood journey. I'm sorry for wanting to rush through the long and weary days. Remind me to embrace the lessons even rough days bring. I commit myself to walking humbly next to you each step of the way in each brand-new day. Amen.

Rebekah

Successful moms know their own issues—
and don't let them become their kids'
issues.

Motherhood brings out your issues—the good, the bad,
and the oh so ugly. Let's get it out there: we have issues.
We all have issues. And, as my husband always says, admit-
ting our issues is half the battle to overcoming them. It's
when we deny that we have issues or overlook those seemingly idiosyncratic things about ourselves that we get into
trouble.

We think we're not controlling; we deny that we still
suffer from having been left out as a child; we think we're
over what was said about us; we really do think we mea-
sure up and we're not overcompensating for that nag-
ging feeling we've buried deep within us. We feel we've
already dealt with the fact that we were teased as kids and
we've grown up to be quite successful. We think we don't

mind that Mama seemed to love our sister more or Daddy favored the athlete in the family, but deep down those issues still exist and we need to deal with them before they affect how we care for our children. Because, trust me, our issues have an annoying way of popping up just at the most inconvenient time—while we're trying to live out our role as the perfect mom of our perfect little children (ha!). We mothers may look like we have it all together—holding our bundle of joy, cheesing really big, thanking God that we've gotten exactly what we prayed for and our lives and families are finally complete, but we still have issues, and if left undealt with, these seemingly tiny issues will fester and boil over at the most inopportune time into the lives of the very children we intend to protect.

Having It All Together

When we think we've got it all together, that type of thinking will get us into trouble every time. Every time. You see, the deeper we bury the issue, the stronger it will be when it comes out—at the least expected time and in the ugliest way. You think you've dealt with having been the only black, Hispanic, white, or Asian child in your class (that was more than twenty years ago!)—but then your child is thrust into a class full of "others" and your tears surface out of nowhere. That's not about your child; it's about you. That's an unaddressed issue popping up.

Or, the first time you hear your mate raise his voice at your child, you get upset and can't even figure out why. It could be that your issues with authority aren't completely erased. Or when your child encounters a bully or gets a low grade or isn't invited to a party, what's inside of you, even what's buried, will come alive. And how you deal with the issue at hand correlates with how well you've dealt with the issue inside of you.

Author Brené Brown once said at a leadership conference that the messier her life is, the cleaner her kids need to look! As if somehow, others wouldn't see our messy internal issues as long as our child looked perfect or seemed perfect. Somehow what is bothering me will go away if Kayla's hair is combed perfectly and her smile is beautiful. How did we start equating the appearance or success of our children with how we are doing personally? How did those lines get blurred and crossed?

My weight issues cross over into what I feed my child and what messages I give her about her body and what she is choosing to eat. My desire to be smart and respected boils over into how I help my child with her big project and even how I interact with his teachers. My disappointment with life makes me overcompensate for my child, not wanting him to ever feel this way. Really? He'll never be disappointed, ever? Come on; we'd do better at helping him see that disappointment happens and he will get over it rather than covering it up for him. But we don't always see it that way. Our issues can preclude good common sense and often cause us to magnify the issue at hand involving our children. I know you must have seen a mom totally lose it over a seemingly small issue. Trust me, that was about a deeper issue she hadn't dealt with internally!

Rebekah's Story

Rebekah offers clues on dealing (or not dealing) with our issues and how they impact our children.

Rebekah was seemingly rewarded with a husband because she was in the right place at the right time. The lucky girl stumbled across Abraham's servant in Genesis 24:15 when she was out doing her daily chores. She wasn't looking for a mate, nor did she seem discontent with her life. She was doing her job. She happens to be the young girl who does exactly what Abraham's servant had prayed for: she gives him a drink of water and offers to provide water for his camel too (the servant, who was on a mission to find a wife for the promised child Isaac, had just prayed to find someone who would oblige him). It turns out that Rebekah was an eligible bachelorette according to the terms set by Abraham, and she fit the bill perfectly. The servant spoke with her parents and arranged to have her return with him to marry Isaac (Genesis 24:45–59). Pretty easy, huh? Pretty perfect, according to the customs of the time. Rebekah had been a faithful daughter, faithfully performing her duties and chores and evidently being kind and helpful to strangers. Now she was rewarded with the prize: Isaac, Abraham and Sarah's heir God promised to build a nation upon. Rebekah hit the jackpot—without even going through extra beauty treatments, charm school, or finding the trendiest outfits.

Rebekah looks like the ultimate good girl. She did everything Daddy said to do. She followed the rules. She got the prize. But even good girls have bad days and meet trouble. Even good girls have issues, even if they are buried deep inside and awaiting a reaction to make them fester. You see, the ones who follow the rules often have secret desires to break the rules. A good girl often has secret dreams but won't express them to anyone—for she wants you to think that whatever you want is her dream. You know the one who waits for her husband, who dreams of doing all the right things, saying all the right things, and living the fairy-tale ending, happily ever after. She eats the right foods, wears the right clothes, pursues the right major—because that's what others expect of her. She did what Mama and Daddy expected of her, not necessarily what she wanted to do. On the outside she looks happy and content and darn near perfect, but inside she's filled with regret and false expectations.

No one bothered to tell Rebekah that life really wasn't a fairy tale with a happily-ever-after ending. You can do the right thing, say the right things, live someone else's dream, be the quiet, submissive woman, tend to the needs of others—and still not be happy. Your dreams don't go away; they're just buried, girlfriend. Your desires don't change; you just cover them up. So when you do get what you think you want, it's never enough. It is almost always a disappointment.

Now, I'm not saying that Isaac disappointed Rebekah, but you've got to think that the promised child (Isaac) was not necessarily a good girl's full dream. A good girl thinks you'll dote on her because of all she is and has done and has sacrificed for you. (She probably has some entitlement issues.) While a promised child—and, dare I say, a promised child who is a male and the only child of his mother—expects those things anyway; don't they come with the promise and the territory? *Isn't this what my mama did for me? Of course my wife would do these things and more.* I can imagine the unvoiced tension in the household of Isaac (the promised child) and Rebekah (the good girl). *I waited for this*, says Rebekah. *He expects me to do what?* Rebekah's midnight prayers were probably cries, as she came to grips with the reality of her life.

And just as life has a tendency to do, something changes and shifts and she hoped again. Rebekah became pregnant with twins—two baby boys, the ultimate in goodness for the women in antiquity. Not one but two heirs to the throne to follow the promised child Isaac. Maybe God would indeed build that nation from Abraham's seed. I can hear Rebekah now, proclaiming, *My God has seen me and blessed me. Aw, life can be a fairy tale after all.*

Two Sons, Two Nations

But only a few weeks into Rebekah's pregnancy, she soon realized again that life is not clear-cut—even when you get exactly what (or more than) you asked for. There's always tension. There are always issues. There's always a fight. And this fight was brewing in Rebekah's womb (talk about kicks and fluttering; these boys were duking it out in their mom's womb). Right in her womb, Rebekah's two sons fought it out (Genesis 25:22). She asks God why. And this time she gets an answer: *Honey, two nations are living inside of your womb.*

What are you talking about, God? (Don't you wish you could be so frank and channel your inner Arnold Jackson from the sitcom *Diff'rent Strokes* and ask God what's really going on?!). Rebekah was carrying two nations—what an honor and what a task (see, tension again). Talk about feuding siblings. You think *you* have to be the referee at your house. These kids were fighting even in the womb. They were destined to be two different mighty nations— what a war brewing inside of Rebekah. Until the delivery, they were warring and Jacob even comes out holding his brother's heel (Genesis 25:26), further foreshadowing the mighty war that will continue as the older will serve the younger. Rebekah's world has been turned upside down by these boys; nothing will go quite as expected or planned. They will continue to disrupt the even flow of life and change the trajectory of traditions. (Sounds just like motherhood, huh?)

Oh, Mama Rebekah was in for the time of her life with two warring baby boys, Jacob and Esau! And you thought your kids were always fighting!

But what did good-girl Rebekah do with her unresolved issues? Did she seek therapy? Did she talk it out with Isaac, her partner in raising these warring boys? Did she pray about how unfair this deal felt? I don't see that in scripture. What I do see in scripture is that she loved Jacob while her husband, Isaac, loved Esau (Genesis 25:28). A divided house continued. These boys were brought up in a home with divided values and principles—no wonder they were so different and held so much animosity. Children know, whether they say it or not. They hear the arguments. They feel the tension. Unresolved issues may go unspoken, but they live on—and we can pass these issues on to our kids.

What caused Rebekah and her husband to take sides and to love their sons differently? Why couldn't they wisely take into account what differences each child needed to grow up healthy and whole? This couple—who were probably warring themselves—actually chose their favorites according to their own issues and each treated one boy as the beloved, favored child. Isaac loved Esau, who was more like him, an outdoorsman and hunter type. Rebekah chose Jacob because he was a mama's boy who liked hanging around the house, cooking and enjoying the serenity of home, especially when Isaac and Esau were out-side, I'm sure (Genesis 25:27).

I can hear—and relate to—Rebekah's rationale: *If I can't get the love and support I need from Isaac, I will make Jacob into the man I wish I had. We'll bake together and laugh about life. We'll speak softly to each other and enjoy each other's company—especially when those rough and tough guys are out of the house. They don't like talking about sentimental things, but I know my son Jacob will—I'll make sure of it. I'll raise him to be the friend I do not have in my husband. I'll raise Jacob to be my companion. We have more in common anyway.*

For Rebekah, Jacob was easy to love. Jacob was the one who was more like her. He did what she wanted him to do; he enjoyed the things she wanted him to enjoy. He was her prince. He was a good substitute for what she didn't get in Isaac. She made her child her mate. Ouch! Watch it, mamas. I've seen it, I've been tempted by it—*Let's go to the restaurant I want to go to; let's do the things I wanted to do when I was a child; let's get good grades because I got good grades; let's be popular because I wanted to be popular.* We can turn our kids into mirror images of ourselves—or the selves we wished we were. It's dangerous, and it's unfair to our children.

Children as Mates and Friends

Using our children as our mates or even friends can happen so easily because it's so much easier to control our children than our mates or any other adult in our lives. And it is especially easy to control a child who wants to please you; he can become your best friend without your realizing it.

But this isn't the beginning of a beautiful bond; it can be a recipe for disaster if we don't watch it. Jacob, whom I admittedly have a love-hate relationship with, is seen as a forefather of our faith. We pray to the God of Abraham, Isaac, and Jacob. This Jacob is a pretty big deal. He was named Israel, his nation. But a close look at scripture also reveals that Jacob was a manipulator (Genesis 25:30–34), a trickster (Genesis 27:35–36), a crooked businessman (Genesis 30:41–43), a person who did whatever he needed to do to get what he wanted, the one who took advantage of the weak at their weakest moment. Yep, Jacob represents the ugly inside all of us.

To me, he represents the controlling mother who wants to make her child be the person she wasn't. Jacob is the controlling mother who makes a child her mate because the child's daddy doesn't act the way she wants him to. Jacob represents what happens when we're tired of playing good and we want to push God's hand and grab what we want, even though it isn't time. (See Genesis 27:5–29 to find out how Rebekah helped trick Isaac into blessing the younger rather than older son.) Although God had already promised the younger would be greater, Rebekah and Jacob used trickery and deception to make him so. Isn't manipulation always about our wanting our way right now like spoiled children who don't want to wait or who don't trust that waiting will yield the results we desire? Check your trust meter if you find yourself manipulating situations and loved ones. It may be time to build your trust and faith in God rather than scheming to get what you want.

Like Mama, Like Child

Jacob learned from his mama. She looked like a good girl on the surface, but deep down Rebekah had real issues of regret and disappointment, and she let them get in the way of raising her children. She passed along her controlling nature to Jacob, and poor Esau looks like he floundered through life. Didn't the rough kid need love too? Didn't the outdoorsman who was so much like his dad deserve Rebekah's best too?

I know it's easy to love the child who is so much like you or the child who wants nothing more than to please you. But the rough kid, the tough kid, the hard-to-figure-out kid, the difficult-to-love kid needs our love too. How does she learn to get along with people who are different? How does she learn that Mom's love is unconditional and not based on her performance and actions? How does he learn to be comfortable with himself if Mom isn't comfortable with him? How will she learn that a woman's power doesn't come from controlling and manipulating a situation but rather from leaning and depending on a greater power than herself? How will our children know if we haven't dealt with our own issues?

Ode to Rebekah

Dear Rebekah, thank you for teaching us moms to love unconditionally, even when it is hard and even when we'd prefer to love the easy child more. Thank you for reminding us to keep our favoritism in check so we can make sure all our children feel our love and won't throw away their natural-born birthrights to become who God has destined them to be.

Rebekah, thank you for reminding us to deal with what's really eating at us, what's bothering us—even as we raise God's precious gifts. Thank you for reminding us good girls that we can't bury our issues and never expect them to come to the surface. We don't ever intend to hurt our children. We don't want our issues to taint our view and cause us to neglect one child for the other or to pass on controlling, manipulative ways.

Thank you, Rebekah. Because of your mistakes, we can learn to love unconditionally, even when the one who needs the most love is ourselves.

———

Dear Lord, help us to love ourselves to wholeness, where we admit our shortcomings and cast our cares on you. Open our eyes and our hearts to reveal

our issues. Give us the wisdom to seek help when needed, ever growing and moving toward the people you've created us to be. We have love to give and we want to give it away with no strings attached. Motherhood is such a sacred task, we desire to have clean hearts and clean minds and clean slates when raising the next generation. We know that this is possible only through you. So, please cleanse us and renew our commitment to loving you, ourselves, our mates, our neighbors, and all of the children you've given us to nurture and guide. We don't take this task lightly. We know the hand that rocks the cradle rules the world—and we want to be vigilant guardians of our hearts and of our charges. Amen.

Leah

Successful moms don't use their kids as pawns in their love life.

While holding our bouncing baby, dressing him up just as we desire (isn't that the real reason some of us celebrate Halloween?!), dreaming of who she'll grow up to be, learning about his quirks can be fun, and the stuff we moms dream about and live off of and thrive on, motherhood doesn't solve our issues. If you've had the privilege to be a mom, you know it's no fairy-tale ending. I'm not even talking about the sleepless nights (when she's a babe or when he's a teen out driving your car). I'm not really talking about the long days of pining over homework and homework and homework (really, another worksheet?!) or the school project that you didn't even do when you were growing up (but I bet you know how to make a volcano now that you've successfully raised a kid!).

Sometimes in life you're able to get by without showing

your issues—no one remembers that you were bullied (except you), no one ever knows that that teacher said you'd never amount to anything (but you), no one remembers your being chosen last for the school team in P.E. (except you), but when you become a mom, it's almost as if those issues were placed on Main Street. It's almost as if we had a sign with our issues written right on it and the entire world were able to read about our issues.

Not only does motherhood not solve our issues, but, in fact, some deeply buried issues get exposed with motherhood. (Read Rebekah's story in the previous chapter.) And dare I go a step further and call out a big issue: our love life! Ouch...I hear it. Whether you're married, single, just getting along, dating, or waiting, love is a big issue for women. And often our issues with love show up at the most inopportune time. Our issues with our child's father can take on a new world of their own. Have you ever withheld something from your child, in some warped way thinking you were withholding from her father? Have you ever overcompensated for what you thought the father should or should not be doing? How about trying to force a better relationship between the child and the dad so your relationship could possibly be better? Love and relationships and motherhood can be a recipe for a big mess if we're not careful.

If we don't know where we stand with love, we're going to fall in a trap and our kids will feel it. As hard as it may be, be honest about your love life. As hard as it is, recognize when it's about him (dad) and not him (son). Treat the issues separately. Deal with Dad as an adult—whether or not you think he acts like one. Express your emotions—love, hate, disappointment, disregard. Get them out. Go to counseling. Deal with them. Find out where these emotions come from—how was your relationship with your own dad? How do you view the male species? Do you have positive relationships with responsible and intelligent men? Do you see them as caretakers who don't need your emotional support as well? Dig in, girl, it's worth it. You want to share your love freely with your kids, not have it ebb and flow conditionally, as it may with your mate. Check out Leah's story in Genesis 29:5–30:24. This mom of the Bible can teach us a few things about being a mom and resolving our love issues.

Daddy Issues

Leah would have been a perfect candidate for a daytime television show. Can't you see her now, saying the only man she ever slept with was her husband, Jacob? *I promise, he's the father*, she could have argued, and the lie detector test would have shown she was telling the truth. *I know he loves me because I've had four kids for him* could have been shouted over and over until a brawl ensued, embarrassing all of us except the audience, who would shamefully cheer on the fight.

Leah had at least seven children for Jacob, who she knew did not love her. She even made arrangements for her servant to have a few for him. She did all of this for Jacob—what she thought he wanted, I guess—yet she never felt the love. Leah learned the hard way that being a mama, having a man's child, doesn't always equal love. Sometimes, in spite of all our great intentions, in spite of all the love we have to give—and do freely give—we are not loved, we are not accepted, we are not honored and cherished. Hard stuff. Real life. Leah's father didn't believe he would be able to give her away in marriage without tricking Jacob (who happens to be a trickster himself!) into marrying Leah. Can you imagine the anger and disappointment Jacob expressed when he woke up next to Leah instead of her beautiful sister, Rachel? After all, Jacob had vowed to work seven years in order to marry the beautiful Rachel. When he did the work, he expected the prize: Rachel. But, because Daddy Laban didn't think his older daughter would ever be given away and taken off his hands, he slipped a veil over her face and presented her as the bride to Jacob. What a setup. Not only did Jacob get tricked, but Leah must have felt like an old rag, thrown away to a man who didn't even want her.

To make matters worse, Jacob is so in love with the beautiful younger sister, he is willing to trust the father yet again and still work to win Rachel. He agrees to sign up for another seven years if he can just have Rachel as his wife too. There goes Leah's self-esteem, falling further into the abyss, only one night after she is married.

What's the solution? Have a baby. (Yep, that's the ticket; works every time—not!) Man doesn't love woman; woman loves man; woman decides to have a child and wishes man will fall hopelessly in love with her and the child. I haven't seen that trick work once. It didn't work in biblical times either.) Leah had lived a loveless life for a long time and thought having a child, becoming a mama, would bring her the love she longed for. Scripture says it flat-out: she had a child because she was unloved (Genesis 29:31). It breaks my heart to read her voice in scripture: *I have a son. I'll name him Reuben because "the LORD has seen my misery. Surely my husband will love me now"* (Genesis 29:32, NIV). Leah thinks just because she has the man's child, the man's love for her will grow or develop. She thinks because she gives him what she thinks he wants—a child to carry on his name, a child for him to hold up and play with and boast about, a mini-me, a child for him to say looks just like him—this will work to change his affection for her. It doesn't.

But Leah doesn't stop there. She has more children for Jacob. More children, expecting the outcome to be different. *He will love me this time.* Can't you hear her cry: *Just one more time. One more child. This time it will be different.* Her children's names actually bear the mark of her desperation—and ours do too. Reuben means *God has seen my misery.* Simeon means *God hears*—Leah said, "The LORD heard that I am not loved" (Genesis 29:33, NIV). Leah's third child, Levi, means *attached*: "Now at last my husband will become attached to me, because I have borne him three sons" (Genesis 29:34, NIV). Doesn't your heart hurt for sister Leah? After her fourth son, Judah, which means *praise*, scripture says she stopped having children (Genesis 29:35). She said she'd praise God. It sounds like she's onto something . . . but don't rejoice just yet; old habits are hard to break, and living a life where you feel unloved has its consequences. It's a setup for using our children.

It's not just children we use as pawns in our relationships; it's whatever is holding us and making us cry out for love that isn't there or isn't there in the form we desire. It's human nature to want to be loved; it's self-destruction to be willing do *anything* for it. And it's hurtful to our kids when we use them in the middle of our love games.

It's not simple to break this cycle. I know it is deep-seated; sometimes we don't really understand its origins. Look at Leah again. She was what the Bible basically calls ugly. She had weak eyes, whatever that means! But look at the comparison between Leah and her little sister, Rachel. The Bible says not only that Rachel was beautiful but also that she had a lovely figure. The lucky girl was apparently blessed with beauty and body. (How many times have you read in the Bible about some woman's shape? She had to have it going on!) Clearly Rachel stood out because of her banging body and looks, and her sister, well, she didn't. Whether or not Leah was ugly—and to what degree her eyes were weak—is debatable, but it's clear this sister didn't hold a candle next to her younger sister. Jacob was willing to work seven years for Rachel. Even after his father-in-law, Laban, pulled a daughter switcheroo on Jacob on the wedding night, Jacob still wanted the beautiful and bodacious Rachel. How's that for rejection, Leah? Will you ever get out of the shadow of your sister? Will you ever have something you can truly call your own? Ah, yes, the children.

How do you imagine Leah felt? All her life, she had been called the ugly sister. And now, the night she thought would be her happy night turns into a nightmare, not due to any fault of her own. Who knows if Leah was privy to what her father was up to? Who knows if Leah knew she was signing up for second place and second wife? But sometimes women do agree to second place. We all desire to be in first place and some of us will do anything to get that prize—even sacrifice the true love and care of our children.

Mommies, our children deserve more, and, quite frankly, *we* deserve more. We deserve to be loved for who we are—beautiful bodies, weak eyes, bad attitudes, mistakes from the past, and all. And the real truth is there's only one way to be loved that way, and that's by a perfect person. The love of our mates can't possibly replace the perfect love of our Savior. Again, who loves us even with our bad attitudes? Who gives us the desires of our hearts even when we are still works-in-progress? Who provides for all our needs, whether we deserve it or not? That's a love that can come only from our God, a nonhuman with nonhuman idiosyncrasies. And the best love I can share with my child is the love of Christ. I need my child to know that even when Mommy is cranky and mean and using her as a pawn, there's someone who won't. Even when my love or Daddy's love is conditional, based on the temperature of our relationship or other external circumstances, there's someone who can give her perfect love. It's not the same kind that will make you have butterflies and it's not the same type of love that will make you want to stay up all hours of the night holding the phone just breathing into it, but it is a true and pure love that you can depend on. It's the only love you can depend on. So when life throws you those curveballs and love is being dished out according to some set of circumstances—and inevitably it will be—know that there is a rock and an anchor you can hold on to that doesn't depend on this world.

Worldly love is nice. Worldly love keeps us warm at night. But worldly love has limits. Know those limits and don't expect to receive beyond those limits. Worldly love can only go so far, even with your soul mate. Know the true love of Christ. Know the true love for someone who cares unconditionally and loves you just as you are.

Look at the lessons Leah learned through her children's

names. She started off naming her children names that reflected her marital situation: God has seen my misery, surely my husband will love me now; he will be attached to me now. But then, before she started giving her servant to her husband for even more heirs, Leah had a revelation. She named her fourth son Judah, which means *praise*. I have to believe that Leah realized—if only for a moment—that Jacob wasn't going to be able to love her the way she needed to be loved. Jacob was a man, not to mention a man in love with her sister. Jacob was incapable of giving her what she needed, but she could find that love elsewhere. Not in the arms of the man down the street and not even in the arms of her strong, handsome sons. She needed to find that love in a different place. She needed to change the way she was looking for love. I see her looking in the mirror, having a long, painful talk with herself.

Girl, what is wrong with you? How many children have you had for Jacob...and does he show you any more love? You could give him your very life and he still wouldn't love you. He loves Rachel. Always has, always will. She's the one who has his heart. Face it and deal with the years of pain and hurt you've felt from being unloved. Daddy gave you away to Jacob under false pretenses—and Jacob still did what it took to get Rachel. She's the one he loves. And having another child, keeping the house cleaner, making Jacob's favorite meal, giving him every little thing you think he wants, will not change your situation. He wants Rachel. But pick your head up. While your husband may not be capable of loving you, God does. And God is capable of turning your mess into something majestic. Accept God's love. Let that love spur you to love others and to love the children you've brought into this world, even though you've conceived and birthed them under some bad circumstances. The children are a gift—in the midst of the mess. Love God, love yourself, love your children—and teach them to love others. You don't have to keep looking for love through Jacob. Accept God's love—and watch your life change.

Leah needed to turn to the God who was helping her conceive all of these children in the first place. Only in him could she find true, unconditional love. Judah means *praise*, showing she decided to stop focusing on lost love and unrequited love and get in with the One who loved her most. She focused on praising God, not on winning Jacob's love.

She still had more children for Jacob after she learned to praise with Judah. She eventually resorted to giving her servant to Jacob to produce kids (as if that was going to garner love for her! Get real, girl!). I guess Leah couldn't adjust to seeing other women (her servant and her sister's servant) having children for Jacob. She needed to be in the game too. So, she had Issachar, which means *reward*. Leah thinks she is being rewarded with more children when what she really wants is love. She has a sixth son and names him Zebulun, which means *honor*. Scripture says she also had a daughter, Dinah (Genesis 30:21). What messages could Dinah possibly receive from her mother, who was still learning to love herself and not to use her body as a game piece in a nasty round of chess with her sister? The madness that we can sometimes pass on to our children just because we are trying to figure out life!

Finding True Love

Leah's story reminds me that as I grow on my journey, I want to be filled with the love of Christ. This is the love that makes me parent well. This is the love that makes me love unconditionally. This is the love that reminds me to love myself as I love my husband, my children, and my friends. This is the love that accepts me for me and loves me for me. I think I'll join with Leah and offer praises for this love. It's the kind of love I want—all day and every day.

And if you're worried about the mess you've made with your own love life, may I offer comfort, even through Leah's crazy story. This sister had six sons with a man who didn't love her and never would. She may have started out using these sons as pawns in her sick quest for love, but, as their names show, she was transformed through these experiences. She learned some lessons as she went through life. And she helped to bring about the twelve tribes of Israel, upon which the great nation was built and we Christians have our origin. All that baby making and all those tears and years of regret and years of seeking love didn't go to waste. No, Leah helped bring forth a nation. God used her craziness and warped sense of self-worth to produce men who would form the nation that would ultimately produce our Savior. How's that for redemption? How's that for turning a mess into a messiah? We serve that type of God. It's a fact. God can do the impossible, even when it seems like we've made one big mess. The Almighty can and will work things together for good when we love God (see Romans 8:28). So our human eyes see a mess and God apparently sees an opportunity. Who couldn't love a God like that?

If you are looking for love in all the wrong places, use Leah's lesson and stop—now! While you can't erase the past and the mistakes, you can wait and watch God redeem you. Give your love to God. Show your children God's love. It's the kind of love that lasts a lifetime.

———

Merciful and loving God: I rejoice in knowing your unconditional love. I thank you for caring about me so much that you gave Jesus for my sins. I appreciate you for making a way for me to be forgiven for every sin I've committed. I confess that I haven't always done the right things or had the right motives—even when raising my children. Cleanse me of anything that is unpleasing to you and create in me a clean heart and a renewed spirit. I desire to live life grateful for the love you've given me and to share your love with my children, my mate, and my community. Amen.

Ruth

Successful moms utilize their village to raise their children.

It's been said time and time again: it takes a village to raise a child. But there's another saying that isn't repeated nearly as much that I'd like to add to the canon of quotes: "Asking for help is tough for mothers." Why? Probably because it's just downright hard to find good help! Or, in real, plain, authentic mom talk: it's hard to find good help who will do everything we say, at the time we say it, just how we say it (and even know what we're thinking and expecting without our saying it). There, that's why asking for help is hard.

In general, as moms, we are used to having control over things. Even if life—or our day—isn't as we've planned, we like to think we are the keeper of the schedule for our kids. Maybe it's because life isn't as planned that we hold on a little tighter to a schedule we can (or think we can) control...I'm just saying! But when we invite others in to help us—whether we actually invite them or actually wait until we're falling apart and literally need them—we have to give up a bit (or a lot) of that control.

You know the drill (or the string of thoughts that run through your mind): If I ask Mom to watch the kids, I'll have to play by her rules, at least to some extent. I won't be able to control what she gives them to eat (for the most part), what time she lets them go to bed, how much she spoils them. I know, we can set guidelines and give strong suggestions, but do we really think she listens to those all the time? After all, she raised us and she knows so much better, in her mind. And we know the mother-daughter relationship is beautiful at times and tense at others. Two women trying to get along, two women with two—or three or four—opinions trying to do what they think is best for the kids. Oh yeah, tension is bound to brew in this relationship.

One of the funniest stories I heard my dear mom share with me and a friend was around the mother-daughter relationship. I knew Mom and her mother had tension; I felt it. That never stopped them from loving each other and caring for each other. I saw that too. (Thanks for the lessons, Mom and Mama Olivia, as you lived authentically right in front of my eyes.) The story goes that Mom, who was always on a diet and very conscious of her extra weight, didn't want my sister to eat a sausage sandwich after school. Apparently, this was my sister's favorite snack and my grandmother quickly and easily gave in to whatever my sister desired. In my grandmother's eyes, preparing a greasy link of sausage in a skillet and slapping it between two pieces of white bread was a simple way to bring a smile to her young grandchild's face. My sister had been at school all day and got to hang out at Grandma's until Mom got off work. (The village was at work.) But there was soon trouble storming through that village when Mom arrived at my grandmother's house early to pick up my sister—too early for the cast-iron skillet to be washed and my sister's face to be cleaned, destroying the evidence of her after-school snack. My mom evidently blew up and told my grandmother if she couldn't give Kim, my sister, an apple after school, Kim would not be coming to her house again.

Whoa, did the threatened punishment fit the crime? Perhaps it did if you considered Mom's fight with weight issues and the eventual health challenges around it. Did my grandmother have a right to usurp my mom's demands? Perhaps, if you consider she was in a pretty rough marriage and used her grandchildren as one of her only sources of joy. Yep, much more complicated than a choice of after-school snack, but I'm now seeing this from much older and more experienced eyes. At the time, I know it was rough for my mom and my grandmother. That's a story I recall often when thinking about how challenging it is to share Kayla with my village—when I want to control everything around her that I possibly can.

And do I even need to talk about the mother-in-law? I've

heard stories. I've seen stories. I happen to have a hands-off, generous mother-in-law who doesn't live close by, but if the tension can be high between mother and daughter, I can just imagine what could happen with mother-in-law and daughter-in-law. Will she think I'm raising my child correctly? Will she try to change what I've instilled? Does she respect me enough to do what I say when caring for my child? I once heard a mother-in-law share that she had put permanent chemicals in her granddaughter's hair during a weekend visit. Huh? Permanent? Yep, the grandmother didn't want her edges to be too nappy—after all, kids were cruel and could tease her. (Sounds like Grandmother had been teased before.) The woman, who was my nurse and taking my blood samples, told me the story, not thinking she had done anything wrong. She couldn't understand why her daughter-in-law was acting strangely and sending messages for her not to do anything else to her daughter's hair. Mothers-in-law can have their own minds. I'm just saying.

A New Model for Women's Relationships

But there is a woman in the Bible who shatters our culture's unflattering concept of women's relationships with one another, and in particular the relationship between mother-in-law and daughter-in-law. Ruth teaches us all a thing or two about the power of using the village. Ruth's full story is told in four short chapters in the Old Testament. It's a great story; treat yourself to reading those four chapters to learn how a young girl's story of love and devotion yielded great rewards for herself and her community. And that's what Ruth really teaches me. When considering using the village, it really isn't just about me and my child; it's about community. So I can actually freely give up my warped sense of control, because it's for the good of all.

Ruth's story starts off pretty dismally. She's a widow within the first act of the book (literally chapter 1; in verse 5 we see that Ruth's husband has died). Ruth is left with her sister-in-law, who is also a widow, and her mother-in-law. Yep, an unlikely trio. These women had no blood relations and the ties that brought them together were no longer there. (Each of their husbands was dead.) Each of the women could have gone her separate way to seek a new life. Neither Ruth nor her sister-in-law had any children, and they were apparently young enough to start over easily; they could have gotten with an eligible bachelor and maybe had a chance of producing an heir—and at the very least have someone to take care of them. (That's how it worked then.) They could have found a spot back at their daddy's home; they were still living in their home country.

But Ruth makes a bold declaration to her mother-in-law, Naomi, who seems like a real piece of work (to put it nicely). It even says in scripture that Naomi wanted to be called bitter (Ruth 1:20). She knew she was bitter and empty and angry at life—so you know she was no fun to be around.

Well, when Ms. Naomi decided she was going to leave the place where she was living (Ruth's home) and venture back to the place she and her husband had left a few years earlier (Bethlehem), her daughters-in-law said they wanted to accompany her (Ruth 1:6–10). Yes, they wanted to leave their hometown and go out with the mother-in-law they no longer had a connection to or a need to be connected to. Both of these women are saints in my book for even considering this. But Naomi convinced one of them to stay home. *Really, it's a better life here for you*, she in essence said. But even in her demanding plea for them to return to Daddy's house, Naomi couldn't convince Ruth. Ruth declared that she would follow Naomi wherever she went and she'd do whatever she needed and she'd love her God and do all kinds of other amazing things (Ruth 1:16–17). Ruth was taking care of the village, long before she had kids. She was concerned not only about herself but also about this older woman who was really left alone and empty. Ruth was not deterred by her mother-in-law's attitude; she put up with it. Ruth was a village keeper.

Can't you see Ruth walking right beside her mother-in-law? *Look Mama Naomi, I don't care if you don't want me walking all the way back to Bethlehem with you. I don't care if my husband has died. You are my mother. I became connected to you when I took the vow to your son— and that didn't end with his untimely death. You and I are stuck with each other for good—so go ahead and pout and try to ignore me, but I'm right by your side. I will take care of you. I will follow you. I will even accept your God and your God's laws. That's how committed I am to you. Keep walking—I'm right with you.*

And when they arrived in Bethlehem, Ruth went even further and took care of her mother-in-law. She made sure she had food (Ruth 2:2). Ruth worked hard for both of them. Ruth was caring about her mother-in-law. And in the midst of her caring, she got the attention of a man whom she later married (see chapters 3 and 4 for more on her unconventional romance with Boaz). He happened to be rich too. And they had a kid—who was actually in the royal lineage! (How's that for a refreshing story—right in the Bible!) But the beauty of Ruth's story, to me, comes in Ruth 4:14–15. The community of women around Naomi summed it up and told Naomi, *Look at you. God has blessed you. He has given you Ruth, who is better than seven sons... and you get to care for her son!*

Those women spoke truth. They said Ruth was better than seven sons. Let's understand how powerful that statement is. You know, we're talking about the times where having a son meant more than anything—and this is from the mouths of the bearers of sons. These women said that Ruth, not even her son, was better than seven sons to Naomi. And seven meant completion (like the seven days of creation). So, in essence, Ruth completed Naomi. Yeah, it was because she gave her a little baby to help raise, but it was also because Ruth didn't abandon Naomi. Ruth could have remained in her hometown, she could have left

Naomi on the journey (because you know Naomi had to get on her last nerve during that long walk), she could have forgotten about her once she hooked up with Boaz, and, Lord knows, she could have kept her child away from Naomi. Can't you just hear Naomi telling her what to do? *Hold him this way. Feed him like that. Girl, give me that baby; you don't know what you're doing!* (Can I just say: I've had every one of those words spoken to me and I still feel a little salty about them. What makes women think they can share unsolicited opinions on child-rearing—or -holding—with a young mother and with any type of tone? Please, please respect young mothers—they are doing the best they can...End of plea!)

But somehow, Ruth found a space in her heart to continue to include Naomi in her village. Ruth looks like she got the prize (Boaz, a child, and child care!), but honestly, Naomi got her fair share of goodness too (seven sons!). Sharing in the journey helped both of these women—and it started long before child care was needed. Ruth took care of Naomi and Naomi took care of Ruth—what a beautiful circle of care.

Utilizing the Village

I sometimes think raising my child is ministry enough; I don't need to volunteer or help others, at least until I can catch my breath and get her into college. But that's not the communal way of living, and it can lead to selfishness, control issues, bitterness, and a stifling of my soul—so not cute on Mama. So I realize that a part of my caring for the community is also sharing my blessing. We've been blessed to have a grandmother whom we adopted and who in turn adopted Kayla. She's not a blood relative, but you could never tell. She has only one grandchild (who is just about my age), and she's retired and has lots more time on her hands than I do! She watched Kayla right around the time she was eight weeks old and I was returning to work some days. She watched Kayla grow. She even saw her take her first steps. Kayla is a part of her life. And now that Kayla is in school, she visits her granny every Saturday. Every Saturday! Kayla enjoys being spoiled by Granny—she also learns to cook, play cards, and be around older people. Granny enjoys spoiling Kayla—and she has something (and someone) to look forward to. And I enjoy a few hours of time to do whatever I please! In my silliness, I used to complain about having to drive and take my child over to Granny's. But, thankfully, I woke up and realized what a gift this was—especially after that day I had taken Kayla to dance lessons and swim lessons, all before noon. When Granny called at one o'clock and asked if I was bringing Kayla over that day, I couldn't turn the car in her direction fast enough. It was then I realized that even though I might complain about my husband's not sharing those Saturday-morning duties with me, I did have help. I had someone who shared Saturdays with me. She didn't drive

Kayla around, but she gave me three or more hours for me. Our help doesn't always come from the sources we expect, and that's okay. Thank God, our help does come. But we need to have the eyes and the heart to see the help—and accept it—and thank God for it.

And if we're going to get the most out of our help and our village, we're really going to have to relinquish our favorite word: control. No, I can't control what Kayla eats at Granny's. I can't control what she does. (I found her jumping on the couch once.) But she's not hurting herself or Granny. On the contrary, she's bringing a little joy to an elderly woman, who is bringing lots of joy to me and giving me a few hours of a break. I can risk Kayla's eating a little too much sugar for that. (Besides, I make sure she doesn't eat any more sugar on days she's at Granny's.) And she usually needs to come home and crash after all of that adventure—which turns into a few more delightful hours of peace and solitude for Mommy.

Village living puts up with complaints—for the sake of the village. Village living gives up control—for the sake of others. It reminds me of 1 Corinthians 13:4–7: "Love is patient, love is kind. It does not envy, it does not boast, it is not proud. It does not dishonor others, it is not self-seeking, it is not easily angered, it keeps no record of wrongs. Love does not delight in evil but rejoices with the truth. It always protects, always trusts, always hopes, always perseveres" (NIV).

When you recognize that you need your village and your village needs you, you can live with less-than-ideal conditions; you can suspend some of your expectations and look at the big picture. Is my child happy? Is my child being helped? When I think about my village with Granny, the answer is a resounding yes. And, as my dear husband reminded me one day after I got really, really mad with something Granny had done: "She helps us more than she hurts us." (My husband is a sage, at times!) And now in hindsight I see that that incident was rather simple, but it impacted my pride...Ouch. Giving up control may impact your pride. Everything you "pride" yourself on—taking care of your children according to your standards—may need to be evaluated every now and then. And I, like Ruth, have also received some sage advice on love and relationships from Granny too! In a moment of complaining about my husband (something I can occasionally do, I admit!), I told Granny my husband was slow. She looked at me as if I had just stated the obvious and politely asked: "Honey, what man do you know who isn't slow?" With a quick question, Granny had helped my anger dissipate and made me realize that my husband wasn't picking on me by being slow—he was simply being. (How dare I try to change him? After all, I've put up a pretty big fight about his trying to change me!) I laughed it off and kept it moving—I was even able to share that tidbit with my sister and we have special codes to remind ourselves when our dear husbands are being themselves. Granny can shed some much-needed perspective on life.

And remember, Mom, asking for help means accepting the conditions at hand. She may not be able to come over right when you need her to. What can you change to make it work? He may not drop your daughter off at the exact spot you drop her off at. Can you live with this? Will she get there safely and in one piece? She won't comb your daughter's hair as neatly as you would have. Will your daughter be okay? Look at the big picture when asking yourself these questions and seeking help from the village. Everyone is an individual and everyone has an opinion and a way of doing things. Yes, the world would run more smoothly and better and more efficiently if they only followed your script and lead, but, honey, they're not going to. No one but you (sometimes!) is reading your script or following those notes you've carefully written in your head. Let it go and let the village help you. They will be happy, and you will too. (I promise!)

—

God, my Creator, Sustainer, and Provider: I know you have given me help on this motherhood journey. I know I have not always welcomed the help or accepted the help because I wanted to do things my way. Forgive me. Show me how to recognize and welcome the angels you've provided to assist me in raising my children. Give me the wisdom and strength to let go and entrust my children to those you've sent to help them become who you want them to be. Remind me to be a help to other mothers too, so that our village may be fortified and we may be a model of service to humanity. Amen.

Proverbs 31 Woman

Putting it all together—a collage of successful moms.

As I closed this review of successful moms of the Bible in hopes of giving us modern-day gals a little help and encouragement, I paused at including the Proverbs 31 woman. Why? I had several reasons I wanted to keep looking for another woman to include in this account—and there are many more throughout the scriptures who could be drawn on these pages. I was tempted to overlook the Proverbs 31 woman because much has been said about this seemingly perfect woman. It's been said that she's a made-up conglomerate from a man's vision. (After all, Proverbs was Solomon's advice to his son.) Who wouldn't want a woman like the Supermom at the end of this book? I want a Proverbs 31 woman in my corner, helping me and doing all she did, seemingly flawlessly. It's also been said that no woman could possibly do all that she did, that it's just not realistic.

One of my favorite preachers and theologians, Dr. Renita J. Weems, got a good chuckle from our congregation when she said her husband asked where all of the Proverbs 31 women were and she replied: "They're tired, mad, or dead." I think she was right. Even my mom, whom I shared Weems's depiction with, agreed. And keep in mind, my mom admits that she tried to live up to the ideals set forth in Proverbs 31. I think she did a pretty good job, but her response to Weems's words made me know that she would probably have been a little less aggressive in her pursuit of this everywoman had she been given another chance. My mom had a deep desire to live her life according to the Bible—and I think that worked out for her. But, at the same time, when women (and men) lift up this Proverbs 31 woman as some sort of status symbol or model for all women to follow, we have to wonder who really benefits here!

But in an attempt to see past the cynicism surrounding the Proverbs 31 woman, I've read those words over and over, time and time again. And while I don't want another woman in life to exhaustingly compare herself to the full picture of that amazing woman described at the end of Solomon's book of wisdom, I do find value in examining her description. If we promise not to compare ourselves or foolishly try to be perfect and complete every task at once, I think we can see some value in the successful mom of Solomon's laundry list for a good woman.

• • •

Solomon begins by esteeming the good woman and wife—and rightfully so (Proverbs 31:10, NIV).

> *A wife of noble character who can find?*
> *She is worth far more than rubies.*

Women should know they have a significant impact on their families—can't you see how they fall apart the one day you step away from your position as mom? They fall apart... so Solomon was absolutely correct when he said our value is higher than rubies or diamonds or whatever precious gem you can name. Sister, you are a gem—not just for all you do but because God created you and gifted you to nurture and raise a generation. You are priceless. And regardless of whether you feel it, you can learn from the Proverbs 31 woman of your amazing value.

> *Her husband has full confidence in her*
> *and lacks nothing of value.*
> *She brings him good, not harm,*
> *all the days of her life.*
> (Proverbs 31:11–12, NIV)

A mom who is also a wife should be in partnership with her husband—and you can trust your partner. She doesn't go behind his back (unless it's for the good of the family and she is using wisdom like Abigail!) or manipulate things (like Mama Rebekah, who helped her trickster son, Jacob). A successful mom's kids can see the respect she has for her husband, not only from her words but also from her actions. She actually holds her man in high esteem; she adds value to his life rather than hurting him. In the end—through the ups and downs of relationships—her husband should be able to say his life is better off because of his wife, the mother to his kids. It's not you against him. It's you and him in this game of life together. Whatever you and your mate need to do to get to this point—do it.

> She selects wool and flax
>   and works with eager hands.
> She is like the merchant ships,
>   bringing her food from afar.
>   (Proverbs 31:13–14, NIV)

I told you this woman was phenomenal. But aren't we just as awesome? Have you seen us work magic with macaroni and cheese and a microwave? Or those skillful sister friends who create even more amazing masterpieces in the kitchen, boardroom, studio, home, and beyond? The Proverbs 31 woman in essence works...and works hard. She's not complaining about caring for her family—and it seems she'll do whatever she needs to do to care for them. She sounds like every mom I know! Even if you feel diminished by reading about her, don't! Your circumstances may seem different, but trust me: every mom I know will do what she has to do for her family—even if it seems unconventional. Work two jobs, quit a job to be closer to home, take extra classes for a degree, homeschool because you're not pleased with school choices, send away to protect him from others... Don't discount your sacrifices. You will do what you have to do, like the queen bee in Proverbs.

> *She gets up while it is still night;*
> *she provides food for her family*
> *and portions for her female servants.*
> (Proverbs 31:15, NIV)

Let me just say right now, imagine how terrific my house, family, husband, and meals would be (or yours would be) if we had extra help—like this woman evidently did. She had servants—with an *s*. This woman was apparently blessed enough to be able to afford the help. And if you are, get it. For some reason, I used to think it was weak to have someone come into my home and clean it— ha! I got over that soon enough. When I can afford the help, I revel in the beauty of walking into a clean home. I once told my husband that it felt like a hotel every time our magical and phenomenal cleaning woman visited. (He on the other hand thought she hid his stuff just to mess with him. Really?! We are from different planets.)

But, whatever the issue we may have with getting extra help—or creating the budget to do it when we can—banish those "I can do this without help" notions. If the incredible, highly touted woman in Proverbs can get help from her female servants, surely you can, if you can. Or perhaps you prefer help in other areas—at one point, my husband and I splurged on ordering fresh meals that I would just have to heat up in the oven; with a two-hour commute, I figured it was the least we could do to try to have healthy meals. Now I'm working at home, and that can give me (and others) the illusion of my being more available, but, trust me, deadlines loom and I still have to do my financial part here, so I'm not sitting around watching soap operas. (Do those still come on?) But I did have to get over my self-imposed guilt when I transitioned to working at home. I thought I should be able to be everywhere, cook meals, clean the house, do the laundry, pick up the kid, get the work that pays the bills done, and be a cheerful mom at the end of the day. It didn't work. Go figure. We still order groceries occasionally (it's easier than hauling bags up to our fourth-floor condo, and it can actually be cheaper because I don't impulsively add things I don't need). We still get the cleaning woman to stop by or order takeout way too much. It's called help, and I'm not ashamed to ask for it or buy it, if I have to. I call it channeling my inner Proverbs 31 woman—because she had help—she was evidently not only resourceful and perfect; sister girl was wise!

She also knows the best time to get stuff done is when everyone else is asleep—told you she was wise. Whether it's first thing in the morning or last thing at night, we can do so much more when everyone else is asleep—and I mean everyone. Know your witching hour and do what you have to do to protect it. Send them back to bed—or downstairs to watch TV or a video or play a game. It's okay; our role model did it too.

She considers a field and buys it;
   out of her earnings she plants a vineyard.
                        (Proverbs 31:16, NIV)

When I talked to one of my former bosses, a good friend, about the dilemmas of balancing work life and mommyhood, we laughed about the ideal Proverbs 31 woman. She's been the butt of many a joke, whether it's right or wrong. Regardless of whether you have to work or want to work or want to stay at home (and work there), the ultimate mom apparently had enough money to buy some property. And scripture does say she paid for that field "out of her earnings." She could have inherited the money, but later on we learn that she sold garments and dealt with merchants. So, I venture to think this woman was so smart and wise that she also had some gifts in business—and she handled them. So, Mom, if you have to work, think about our girl and how she handled her business. If you stay home, I know you're still managing an entire household. Like the Proverbs 31 woman, you do what you have to do to get the job done and to care for those around you.

> *She sets about her work vigorously;*
> *her arms are strong for her tasks.*
> *She sees that her trading is profitable,*
> *and her lamp does not go out at night.*
> (Proverbs 31:17–18, NIV)

Our mom is evidently working hard—even with all her servants! She knows when something works and when something doesn't—and when it's profitable, she presses Repeat and makes more for her family and community. She is the epitome of multitasking (not time slicing, I bet!), and apparently her arms show her strength for they are "strong." (Girlfriend doesn't need the gym to get Michelle Obama arms—she's got her work. Who said manual labor was for men?)

> *In her hand she holds the distaff*
> *and grasps the spindle with her fingers.*
> *She opens her arms to the poor*
> *and extends her hands to the needy.*
> (Proverbs 31:19–20, NIV)

Yeah, she's perfect. Not only does the Proverbs 31 woman treat her family well, make profitable deals, and run her home and outside businesses, but she also helps others. Isn't that what we're really called to do? Our blessings are not just for us and our family. We don't profit just to make more money to keep to ourselves and grow our storehouses. (See Luke 12:13–21 for a story of a rich man who saved up just for himself.) We are called to show the love of Christ through our actions—and how we treat those with less shows how we'd treat God (see Matthew 25:40). Even with so much going on in our lives, we still have time and room to help someone in need. It's a great model for our kids to see.

> *When it snows, she has no fear for her household;*
> *for all of them are clothed in scarlet.*
> *She makes coverings for her bed;*
> *she is clothed in fine linen and purple.*
> (Proverbs 31:21–22, NIV)

This woman is ahead of the game. Nothing is going to sneak up on her—not cold weather or a storm or a growth spurt. She's planned it out and she has clothing for her family ready and waiting. She has covers to keep them warm at night. Did she chop wood too? She is everywoman.

> *Her husband is respected at the city gate,*
> *where he takes his seat among the elders of the land.*
> (Proverbs 31:23, NIV)

Apparently she has good taste in men too. Her hubby is well respected in the city. He too, evidently, takes care of business. Isn't a marriage partnership so much better when each person is doing his best? Iron really can sharpen iron (Proverbs 27:17).

She makes linen garments and sells them,
and supplies the merchants with sashes.
She is clothed with strength and dignity;
she can laugh at the days to come.
(Proverbs 31:24–25, NIV)

Again, our businesswoman is doing things and creating things and making life happen, for her and her family. She is seen as strong and noble and dignified. Can't you see her walking among the merchants? She stands ahead of the rest because she's got this. She is confident. She reminds me of Maya Angelou's "Phenomenal Woman."

She speaks with wisdom,
and faithful instruction is on her tongue.
She watches over the affairs of her household
and does not eat the bread of idleness.
(Proverbs 31:26–27, NIV)

Now we get to the heart of what makes this amazing woman tick. She apparently knows wisdom and the word of God—where else could she get this wisdom? She teaches it to her family honorably and faithfully. I know we have a lot going on, but we can't neglect the teaching of God's principles, in word or in action. We need to be like Sarah, learning to balance our faith with our actions, as our family observes our actions and our instructions.

But every time I read the phrase about our phenomenal Proverbs 31 woman, "does not eat the bread of idleness," I pause just a moment. I personally don't subscribe to the idleness issue. Ever seen an idle mom? I just think we have too much going on anyway, and if we find the time to be idle—to do absolutely nothing but sit and gather ourselves—I'd say take the opportunity, honey. Soon enough, your moment of peace will be interrupted with a question, a need, or a want. And some women will confess that they thought playing with their kids, laughing with their kids, or simply sitting still with their kids was considered being idle. Have you ever seen how delighted your child is to have your undivided attention? It may feel like we're doing nothing, but we're not only giving quality time to our loved ones; we are also modeling how to sit and be…a lesson we modern-day folk can all use a little more in our lives.

But upon further investigation, I think the point of the "idle" verse in scripture is that this woman, as most of us do, takes care of business. We don't let things slip and our families can count on us. No wonder Mother's Day is such a big deal—it should be.

Her children arise and call her blessed;
her husband also, and he praises her:
"Many women do noble things,
but you surpass them all."
                    (Proverbs 31:28–29, NIV)

And speaking of Mother's Day—our children and mates should arise and bless us and our efforts—it's only right to say thank you to the woman who sacrifices so much. Even if you don't have anyone teaching your kids how to give gifts, you can do it. They can make you and Grandma and other loving mothers cards and gifts. They can save a portion of their money for gifts. It's not self-centered to accept gifts from your kids. It's teaching them to be grateful and to say thank you—Christian principles!

Charm is deceptive, and beauty is fleeting;
but a woman who fears the LORD is to be praised.
Honor her for all that her hands have done,
and let her works bring her praise at the city gate.
                    (Proverbs 31:30–31, NIV)

And at the crux of the issue is what's really inside this beautiful woman. Some of us can get by on our charm; others may be able to gain some advantage through our beauty. But those things don't last. People find out about charm easily; and trust me, beauty fades away. (Journalist Andy Rooney once said we're our prettiest at twenty-one...he was probably right, unless you account for the fact that when you're older you have more money for enhancements!) But when you have an internal beauty—one that comes from your spirit—that can last forever. When you're fueled by God's spirit to do this job, you can emit a sweetness and strength that is beyond understanding. When we as moms rely on God for wisdom and help, even when we might feel like sleeping in or quitting or escaping, we can be renewed. We can run like eagles and we can find renewed strength to keep on going one more day. We can personify Isaiah 40:31: "But those who hope in the LORD will renew their strength. They will soar on wings like eagles; they will run and not grow weary, they will walk and not be faint" (NIV).

When we place our hope and trust in God, we can live like the prayerful Hannah, knowing God hears our uttered and unexpressed prayers; when we put our trust and hope in God, we can stand up to whatever evil tries to take our children, as Jochebed did; when we put our hope and trust in God, we can have the peace and calmness that surpasses even our own understanding (Philippians 4:7), like Mary. When we trust God, we can get our love life and other relationships together so they will not interfere with our relationships with our children, as Leah's did. And no matter how long it takes, we know God's promises are true and we can trust them to come to pass, as Elizabeth did. We can wait with anticipation for God to deliver for us and our families. We can be creative and figure out how to make ends meet and continue to take care of our dear ones, like our phenomenal Proverbs 31 sister.

We have all we need to be successful—and it's found in the Word of God, in the examples of the beautiful women we can call sisters.

Regardless of their mistakes, they kept going. Regardless of their trials and circumstances, they did it. They raised their children and found themselves. They sacrificed and showed them their faith. They did it. And so are you doing it.

God bless moms, a child's first love and first example of unconditional love. Our jobs are not in vain. Our calling is not a mistake. We are not alone. God hears and God sees a mother's heart. Sit back and watch God surprise even you, Mommy!

⁓

Gracious and Most Holy God: Give me the strength to do the best I can as Mommy. Give me the wisdom to seek you for all things—and to seek your guidance in raising the children you've entrusted to me. I don't feel as perfect as the Proverbs 31 woman—and I know that that is okay. You're seeking my heart, not my perfection. Turn my heart and mind toward you as I perform each task. Remind me that I'm in service to you as I serve my family. I gratefully accept each challenge of motherhood, knowing you are my provider and sustainer. I look forward to all that my children's lives hold as I wait to see how you will surprise me as I journey on as Mom. My life has been forever changed because I am called Mommy. I am thankful. I am grateful. I am blessed. Amen.

Acknowledgments

I'd like to acknowledge some VIPs who helped make this book a reality. My editor, mentor, and friend Adrienne Ingrum is really the best (and that's not a cliché). I consider it pure joy to work with you on any project. Alexa (Lexi) Smail, acquisitions, has always been very helpful, supportive, and on point. The entire Hachette/Faith Words team, including Carolyn Kurek, Bob Castillo, JuLee Brand, and Melissa Mathlin, has been a delight to work with. I'm grateful for your trust and support.

To my husband, Derrick D. Patton, who urged me to start writing books a long time ago; and my daughter, Kayla, who gives me some really good material. To the moms at Cambridge School of Chicago—our conversations helped me write this book—and all the other great mommy friends I have. I am so thankful I get to be a mom and I get to write about it. And most importantly, I thank God for the opportunity to share wisdom from our road map, the Holy Bible.